Carl Vierow

Detective at Red Castle Pier and Other Drawings

New Drawing

June 2011

Victory Hall Press

Editor: James Pustorino

ISBN-13:
978-0615484754

ISBN-10:
0615484751

Victory Hall Inc. P O Box 324
Jersey City, NJ 07303-0324
www.victoryhall.org

THIS PROGRAM IS MADE POSSIBLE IN PART BY FUNDS
FROM THE NEW JERSEY STATE COUNCIL ON THE ARTS/
DEPARTMENT OF STATE, A PARTNER AGENCY OF THE
NATIONAL ENDOWMENT FOR THE ARTS, ADMINISTERED BY
THE HUDSON COUNTY OFFICE OF CULTURAL AND HERI-
TAGE AFFAIRS, THOMAS A. DEGISE, COUNTY EXECUTIVE,
AND THE BOARD OF CHOSEN FREEHOLDERS.

Carl Vierow

Detective at Red Castle Pier and Other Drawings

NEW DRAWING   VICTORY HALL PRESS

for Dayle, Elise, and Finola

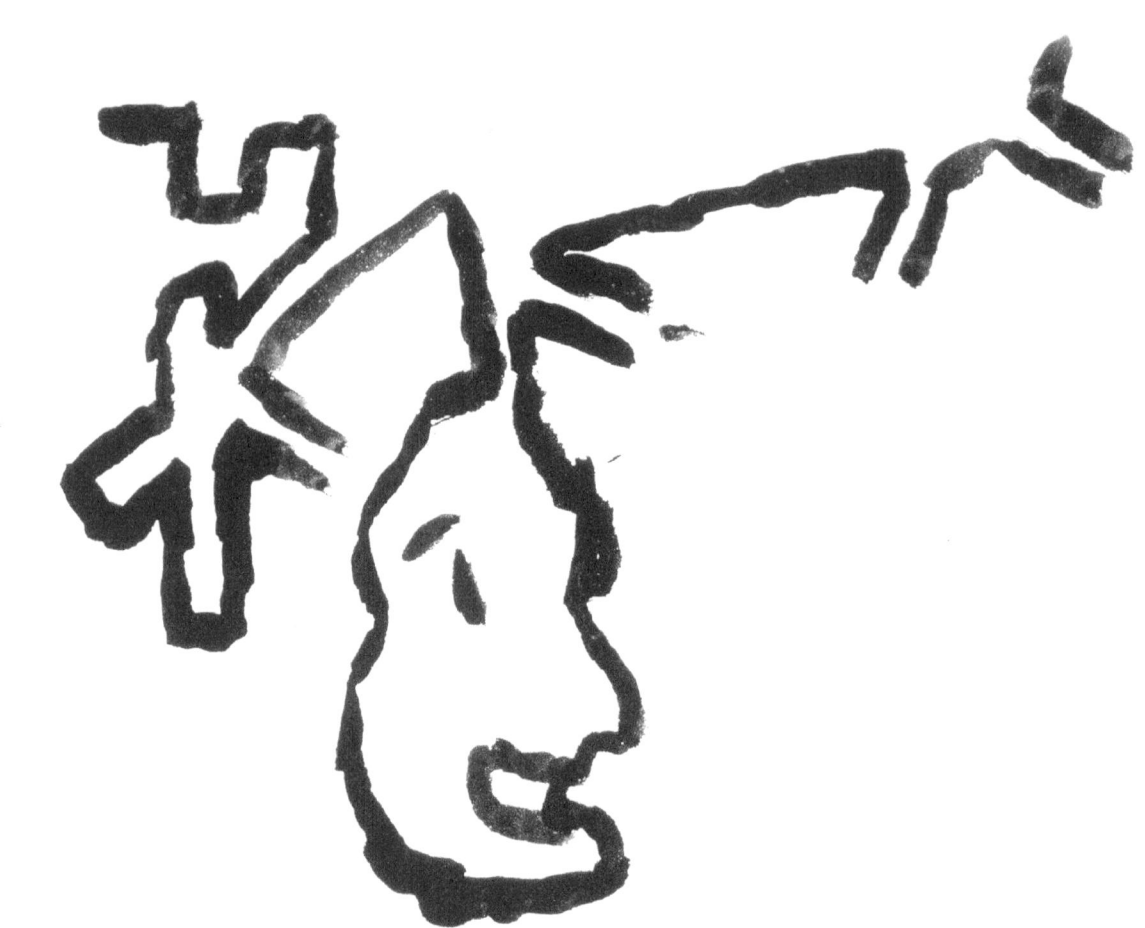

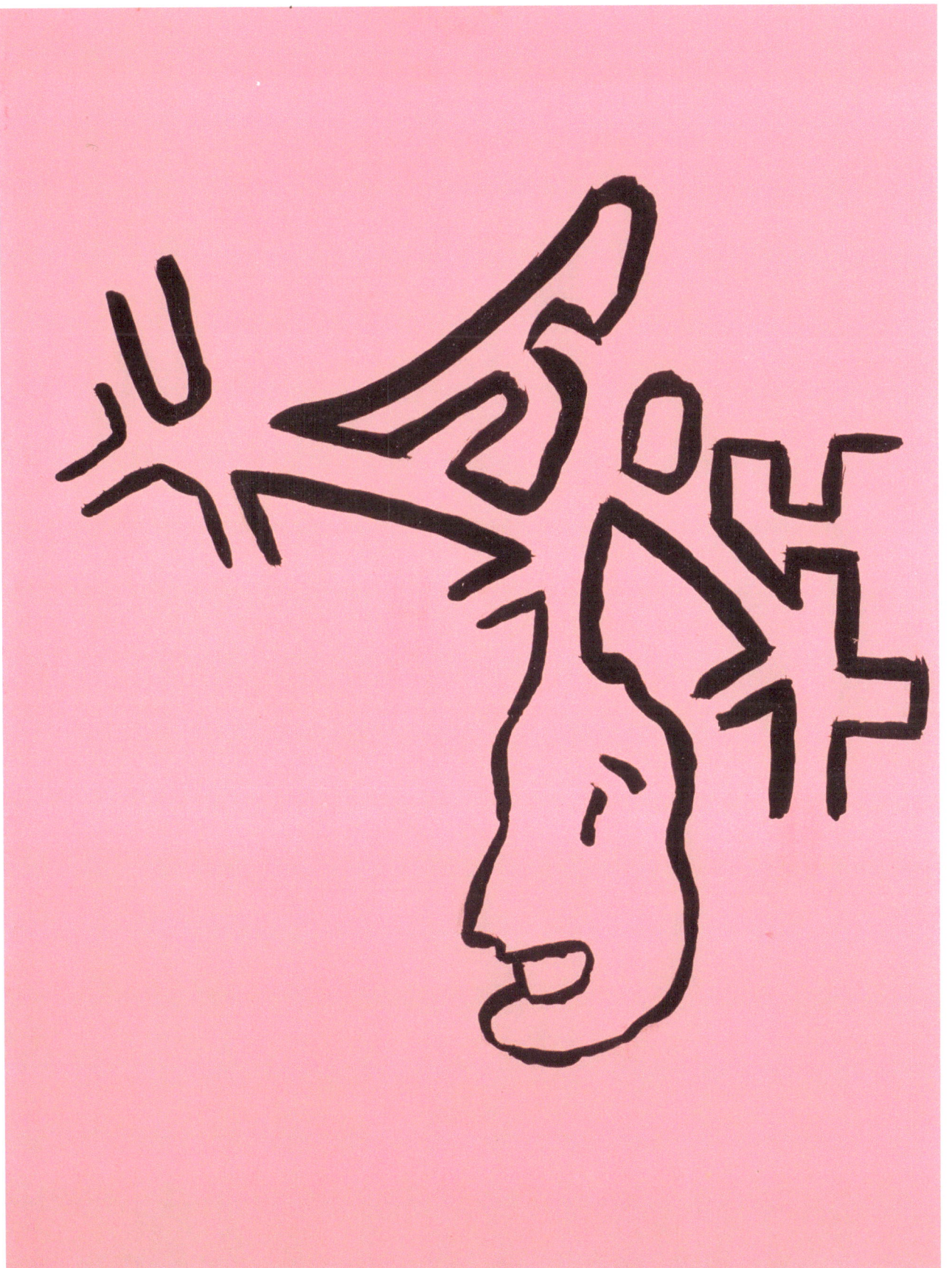

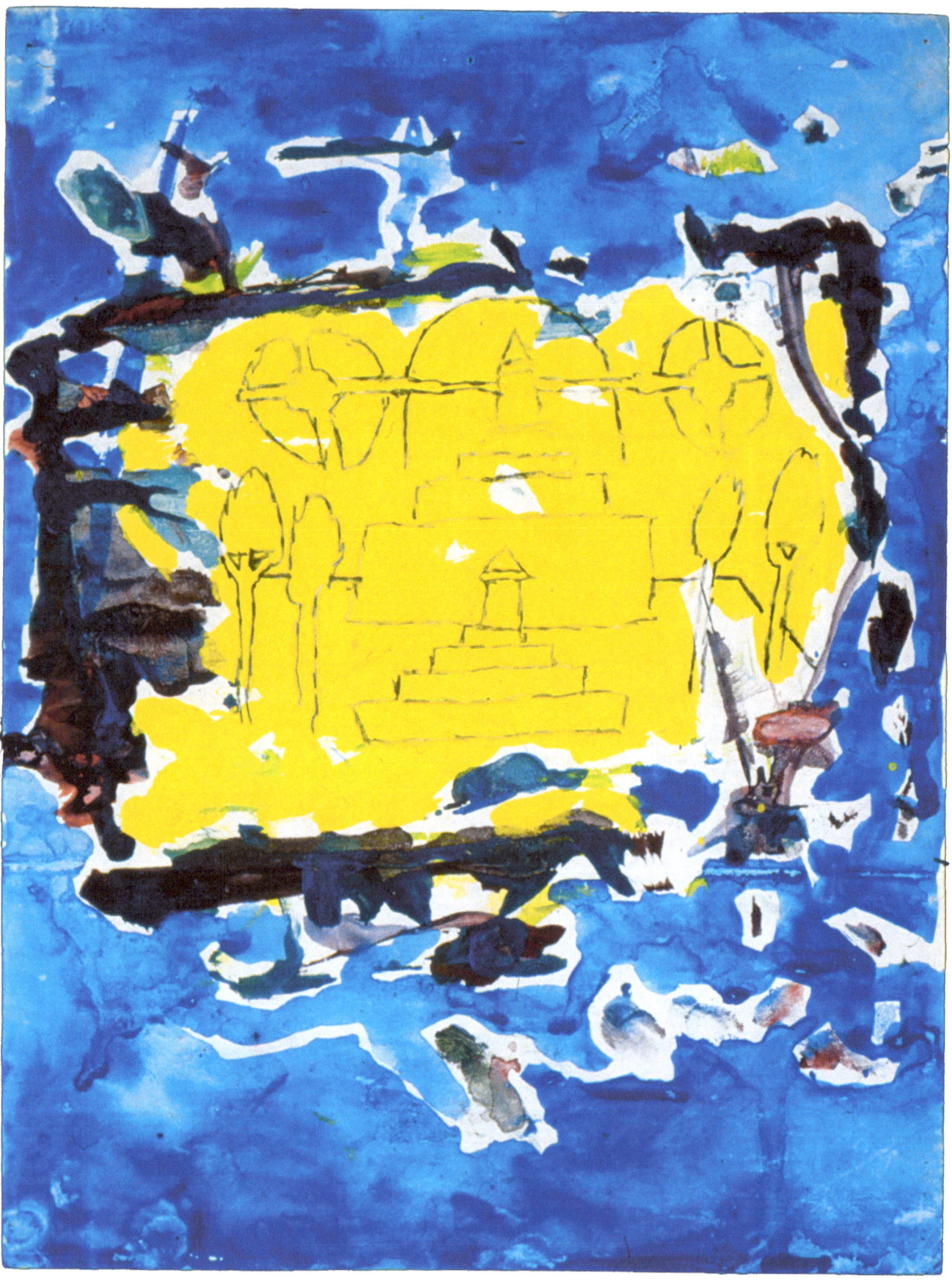

4

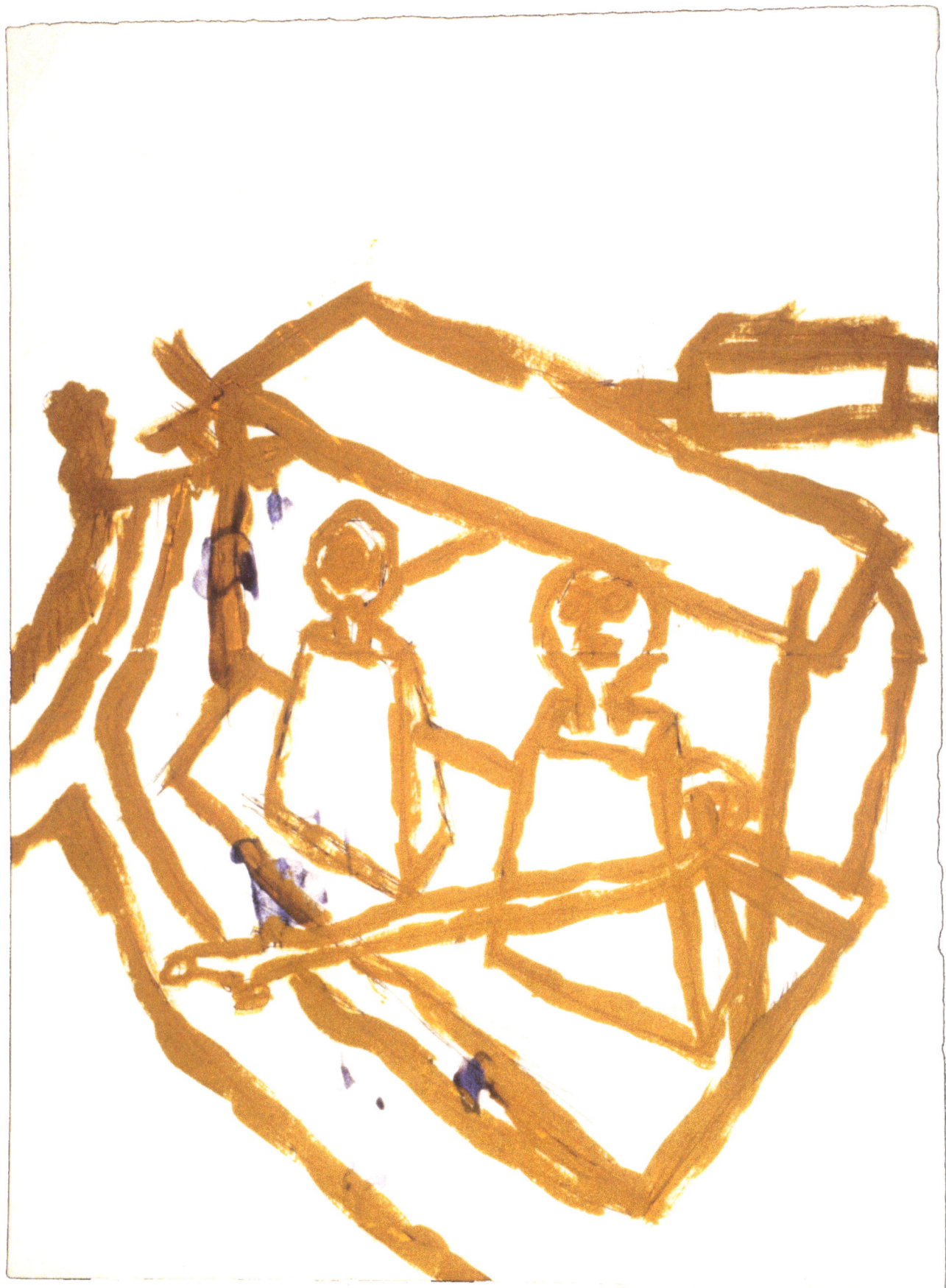

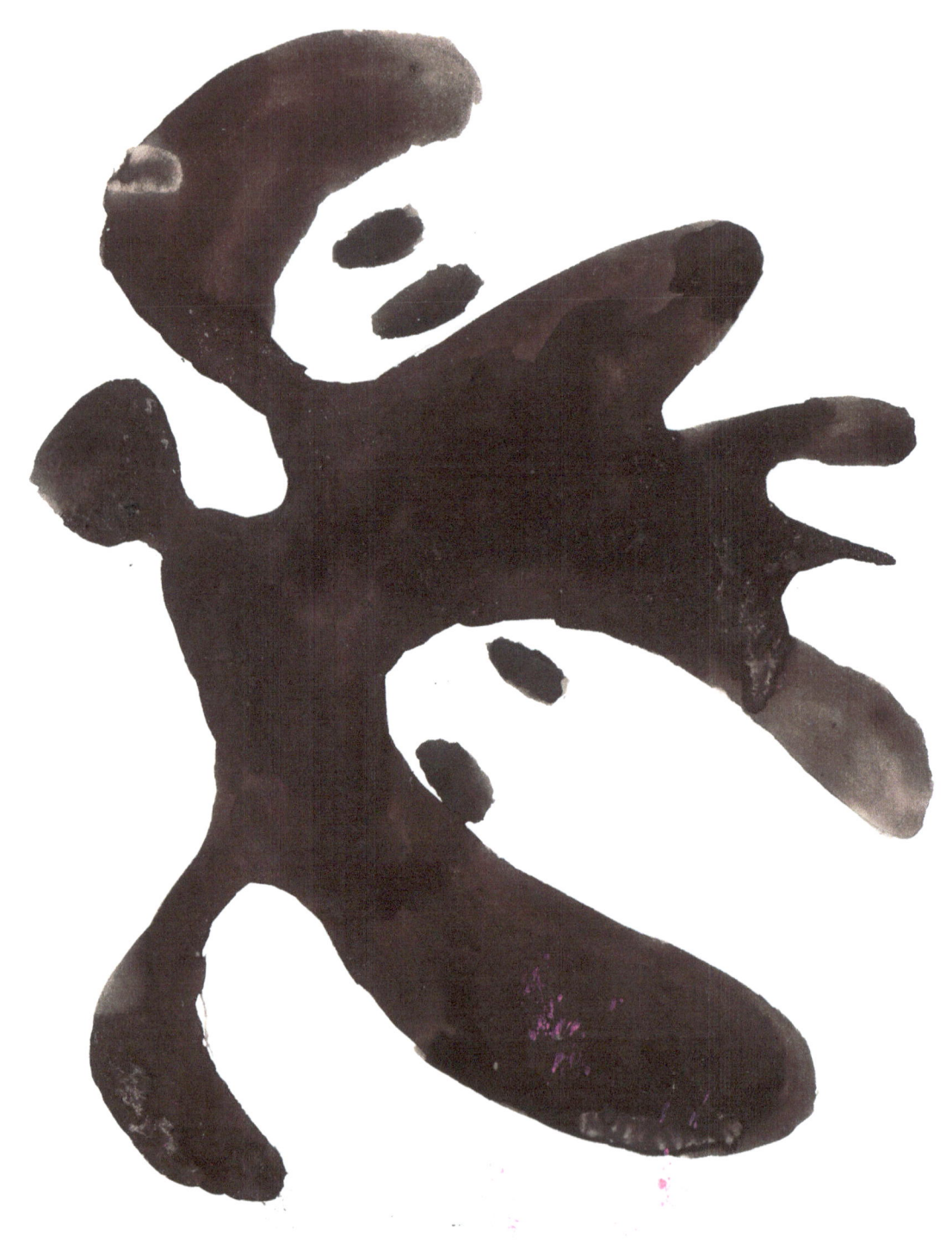

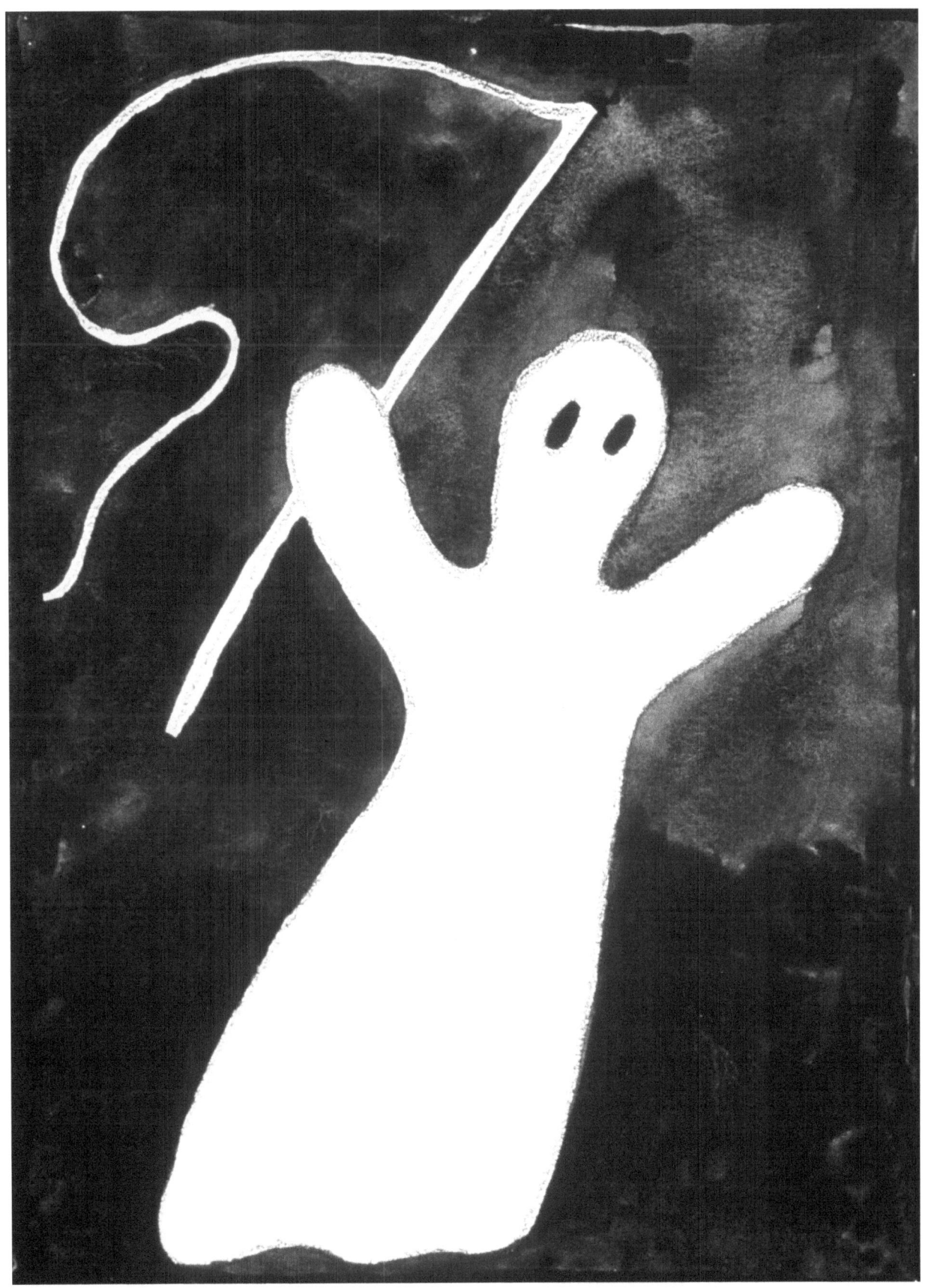

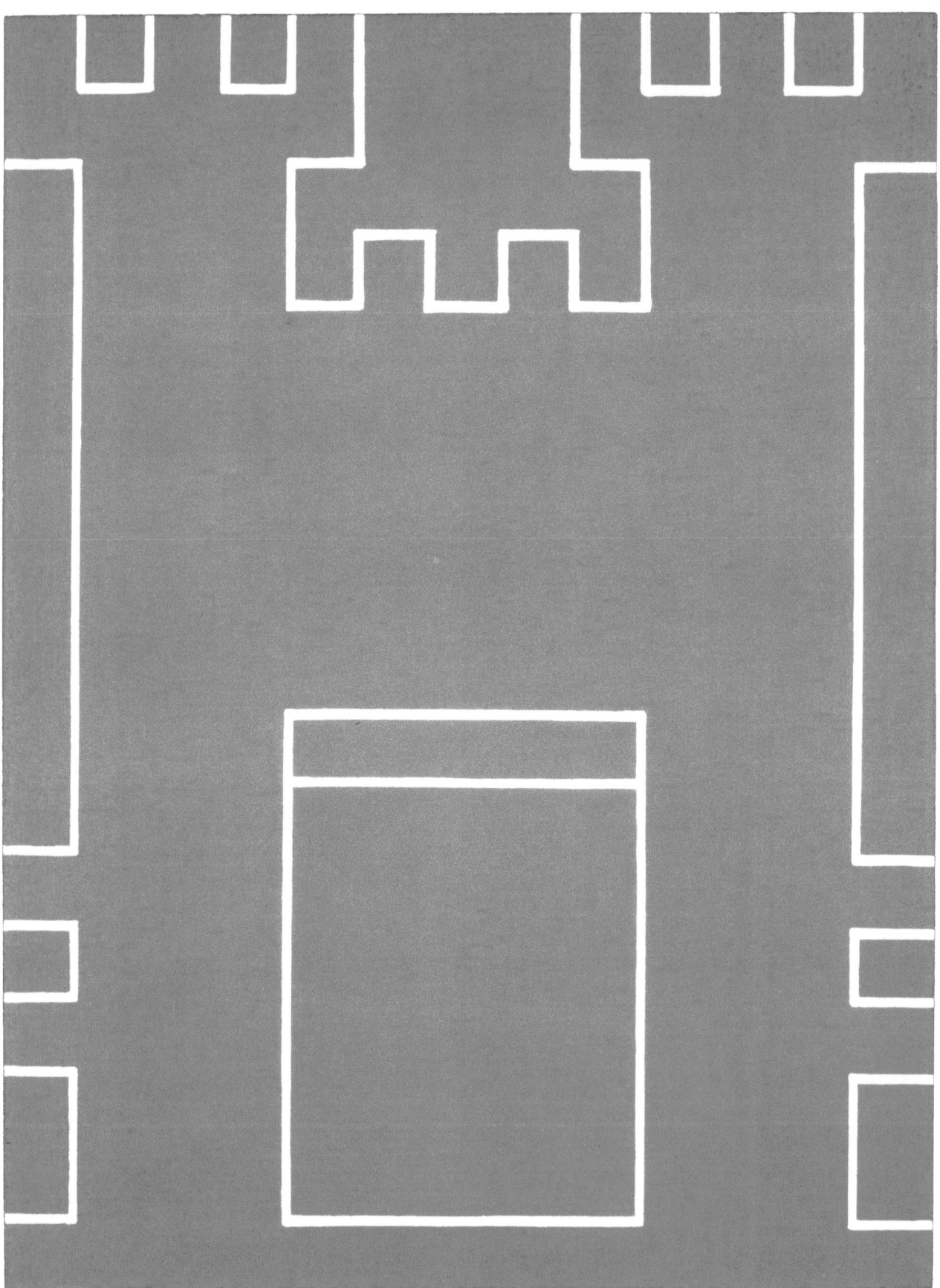

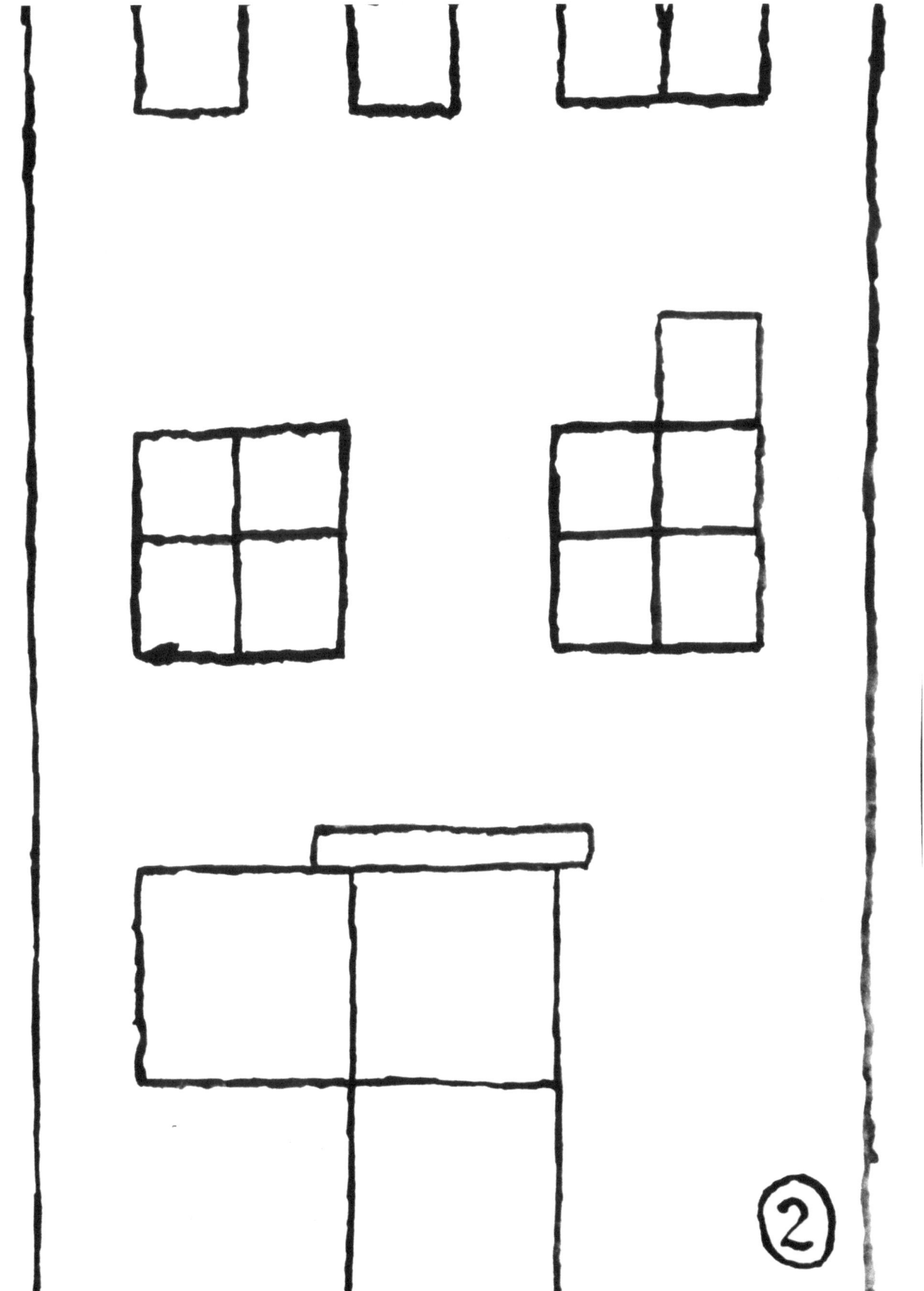

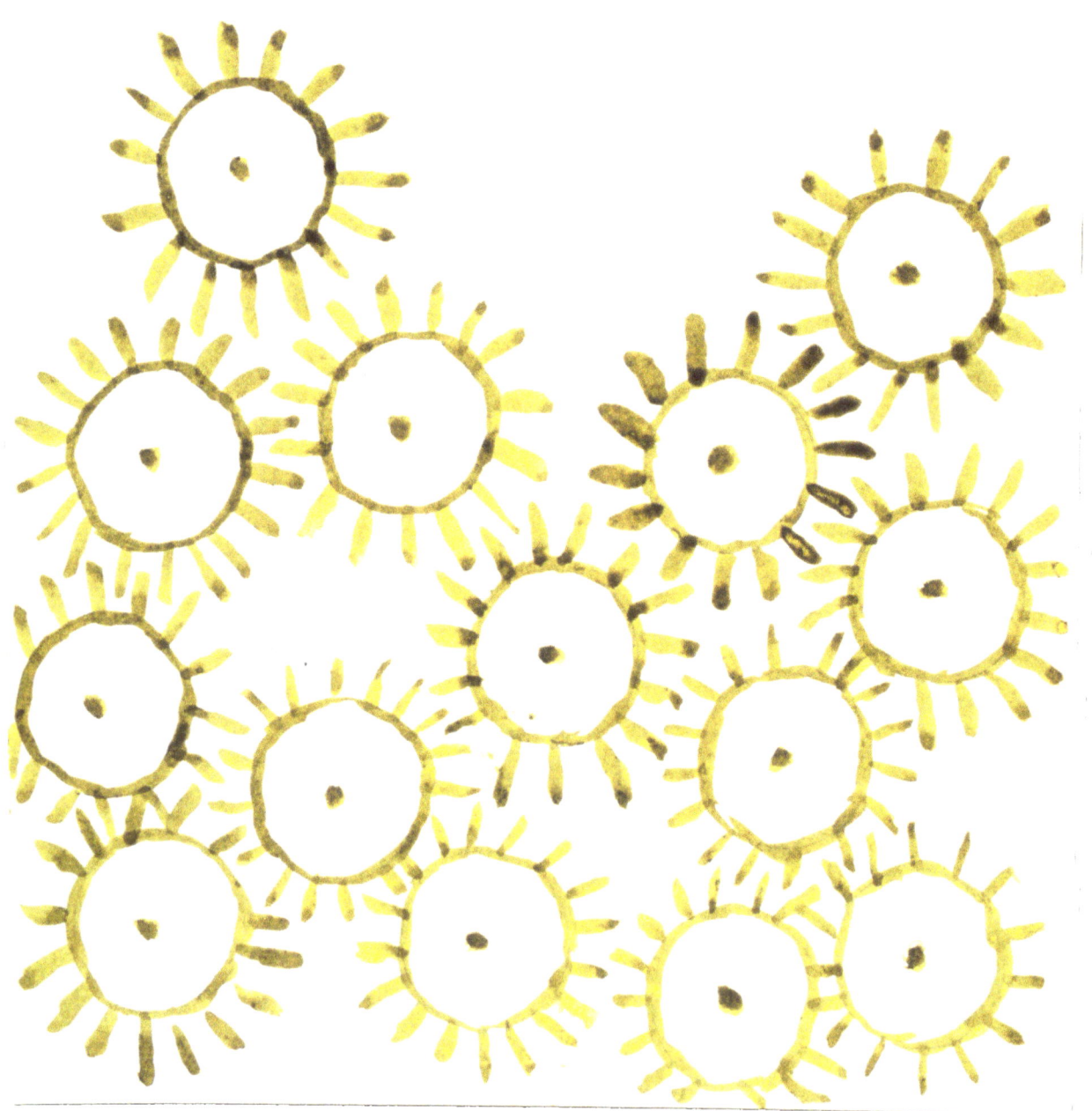

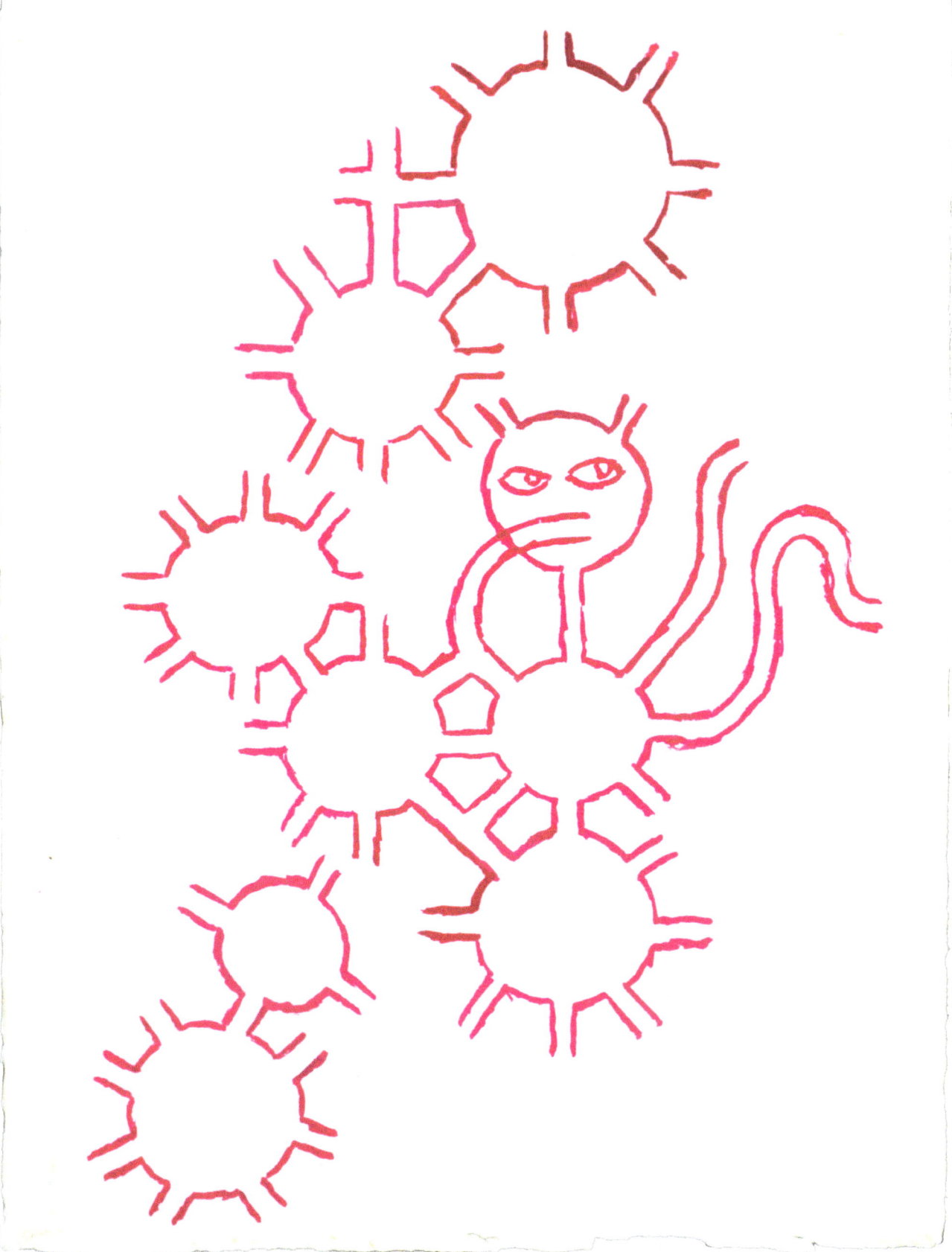

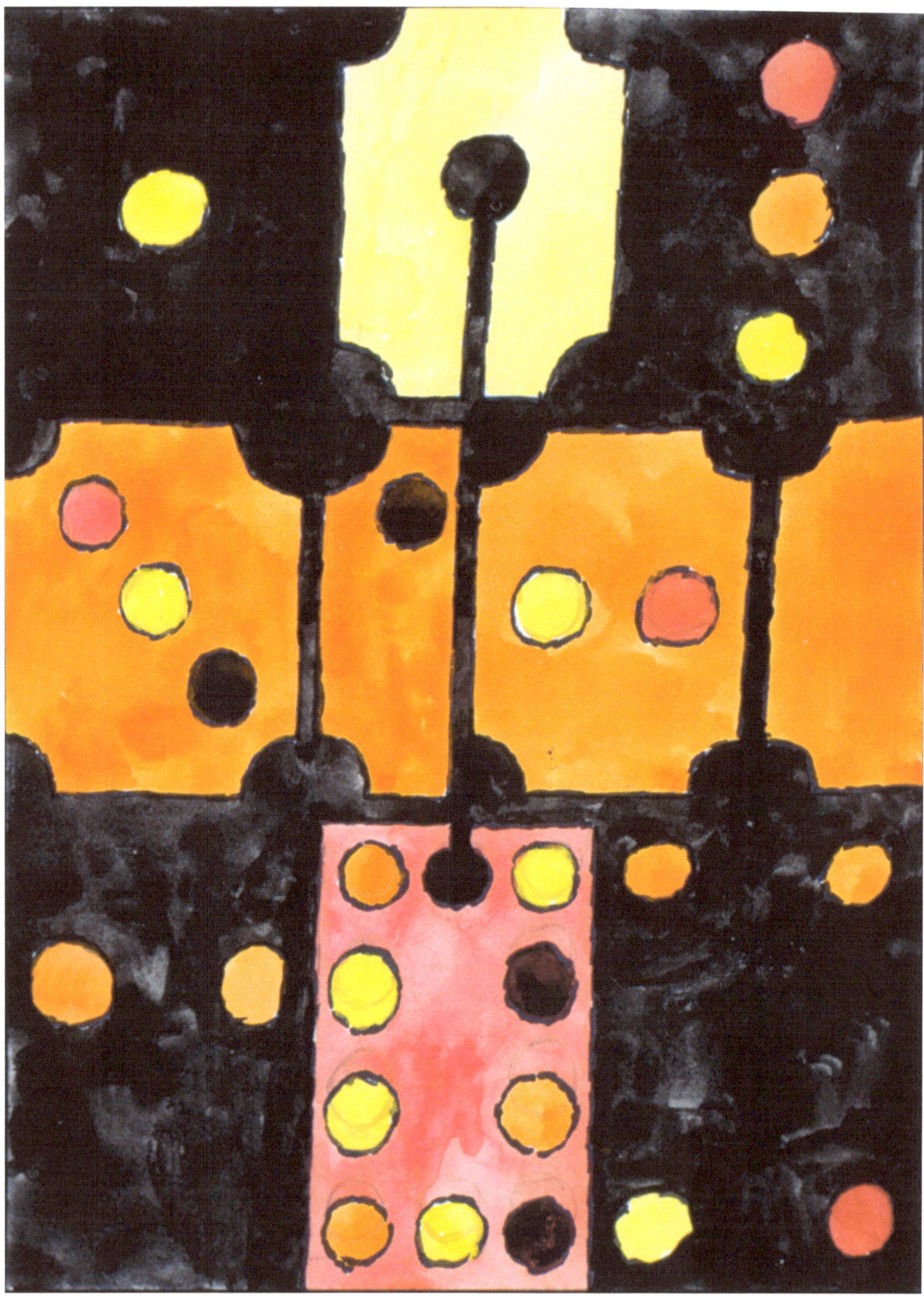

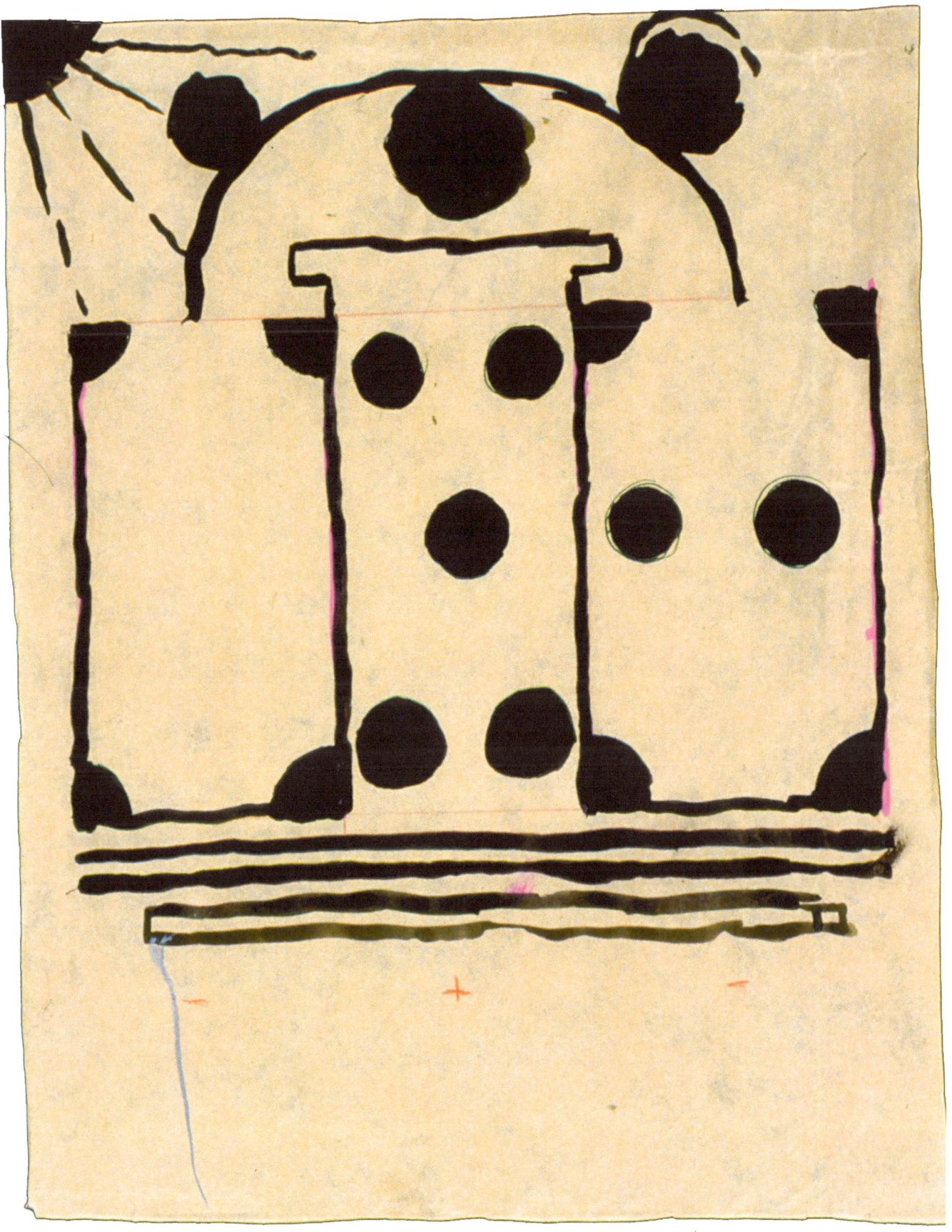

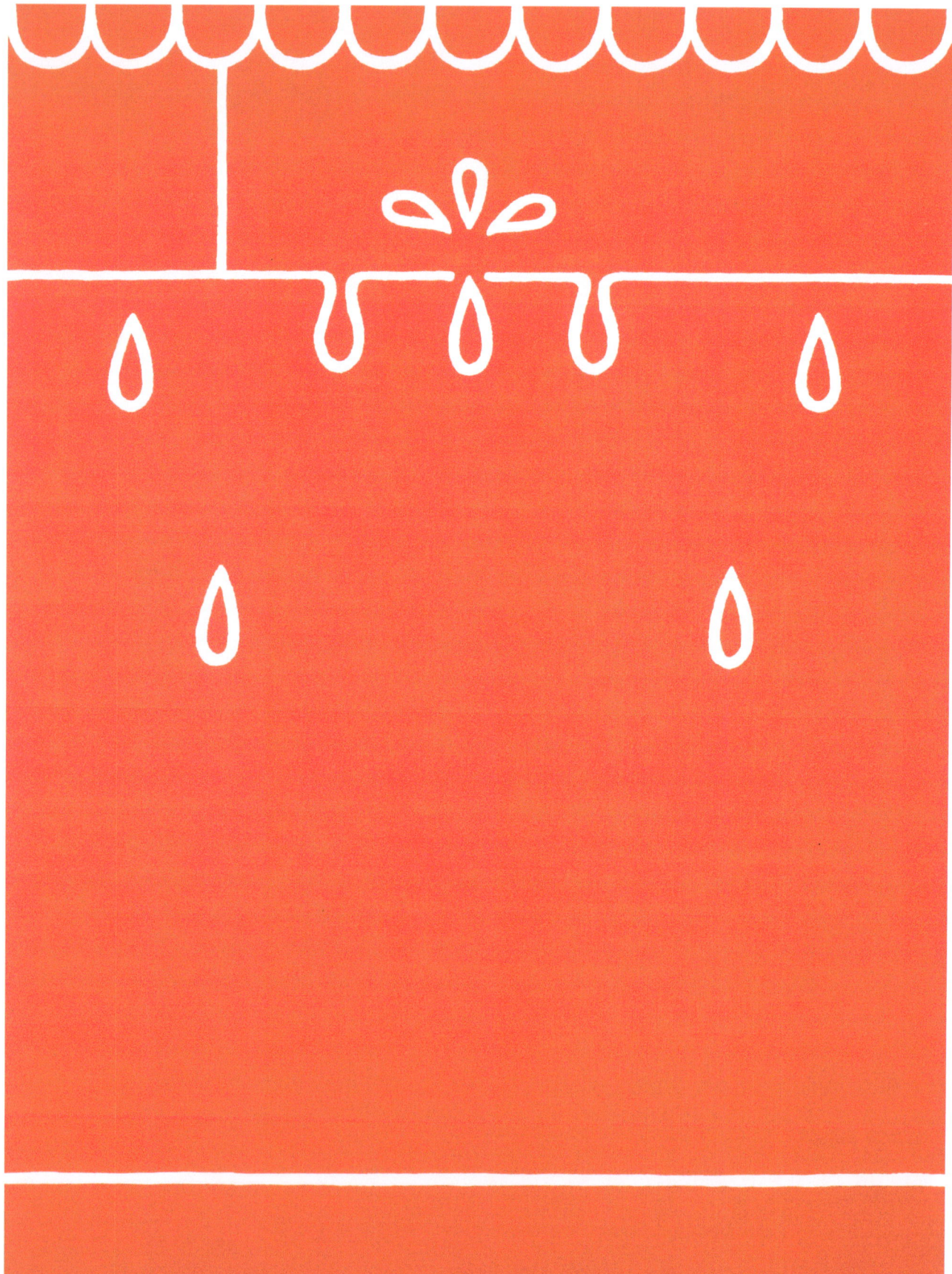

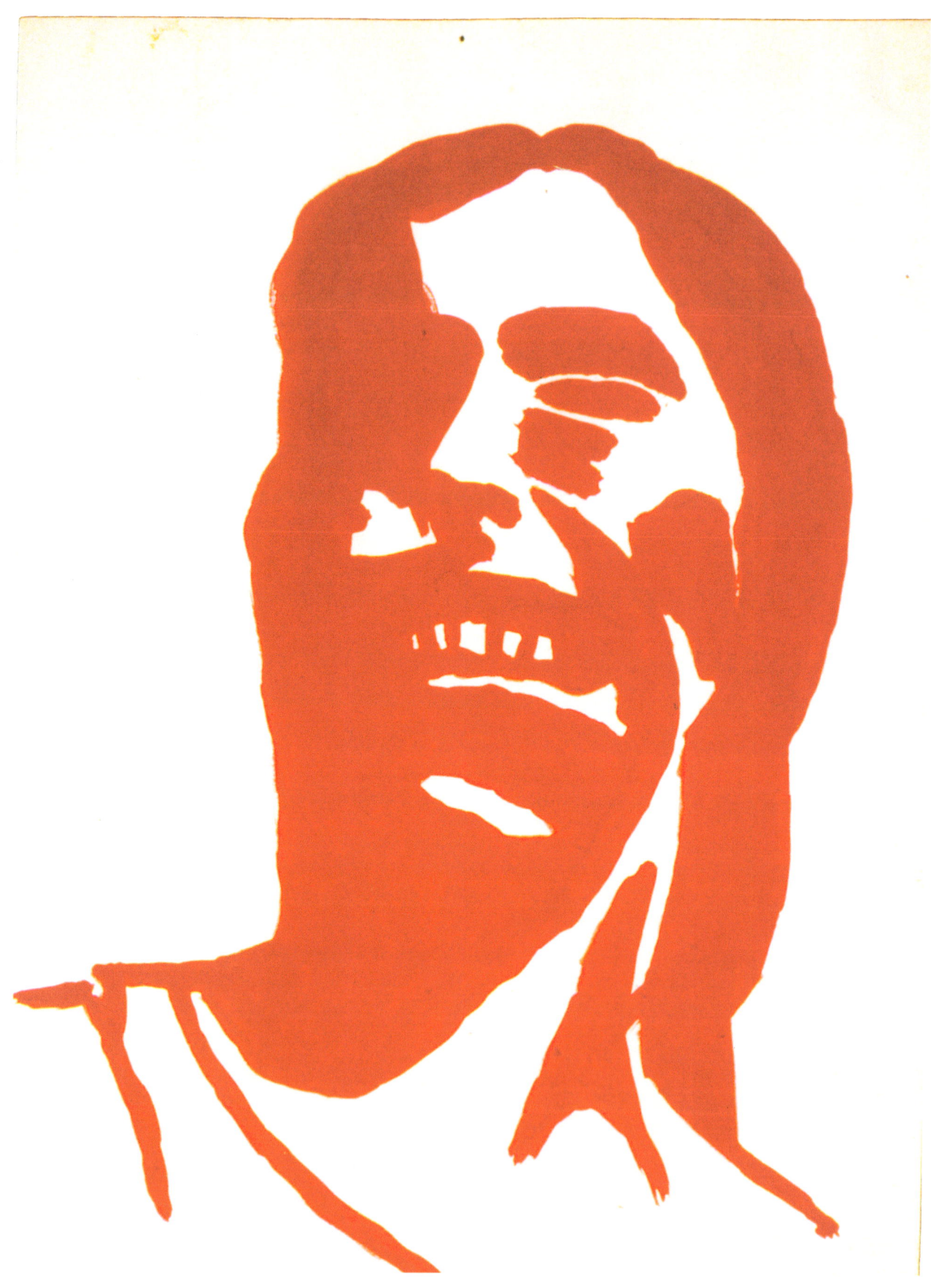

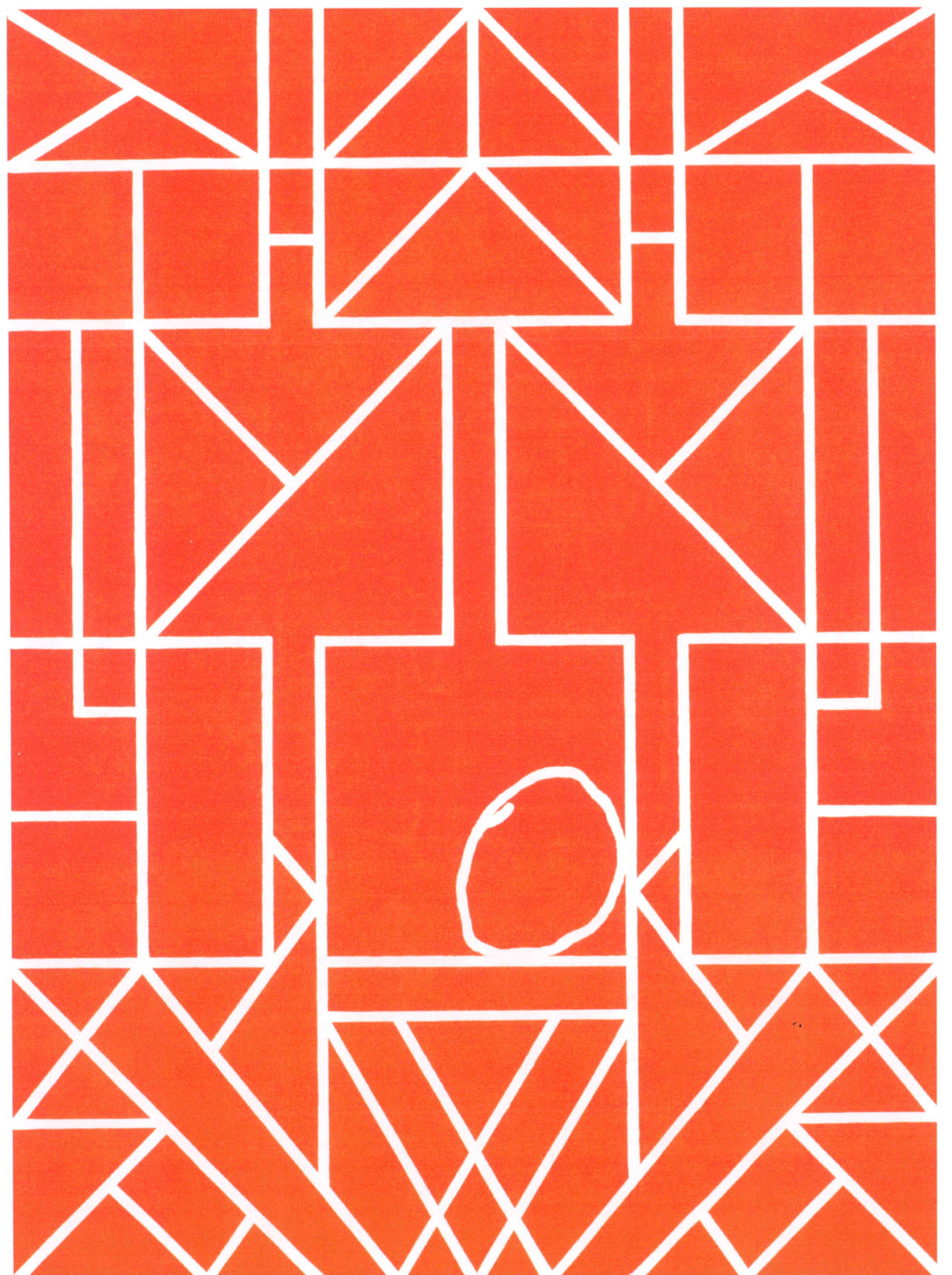

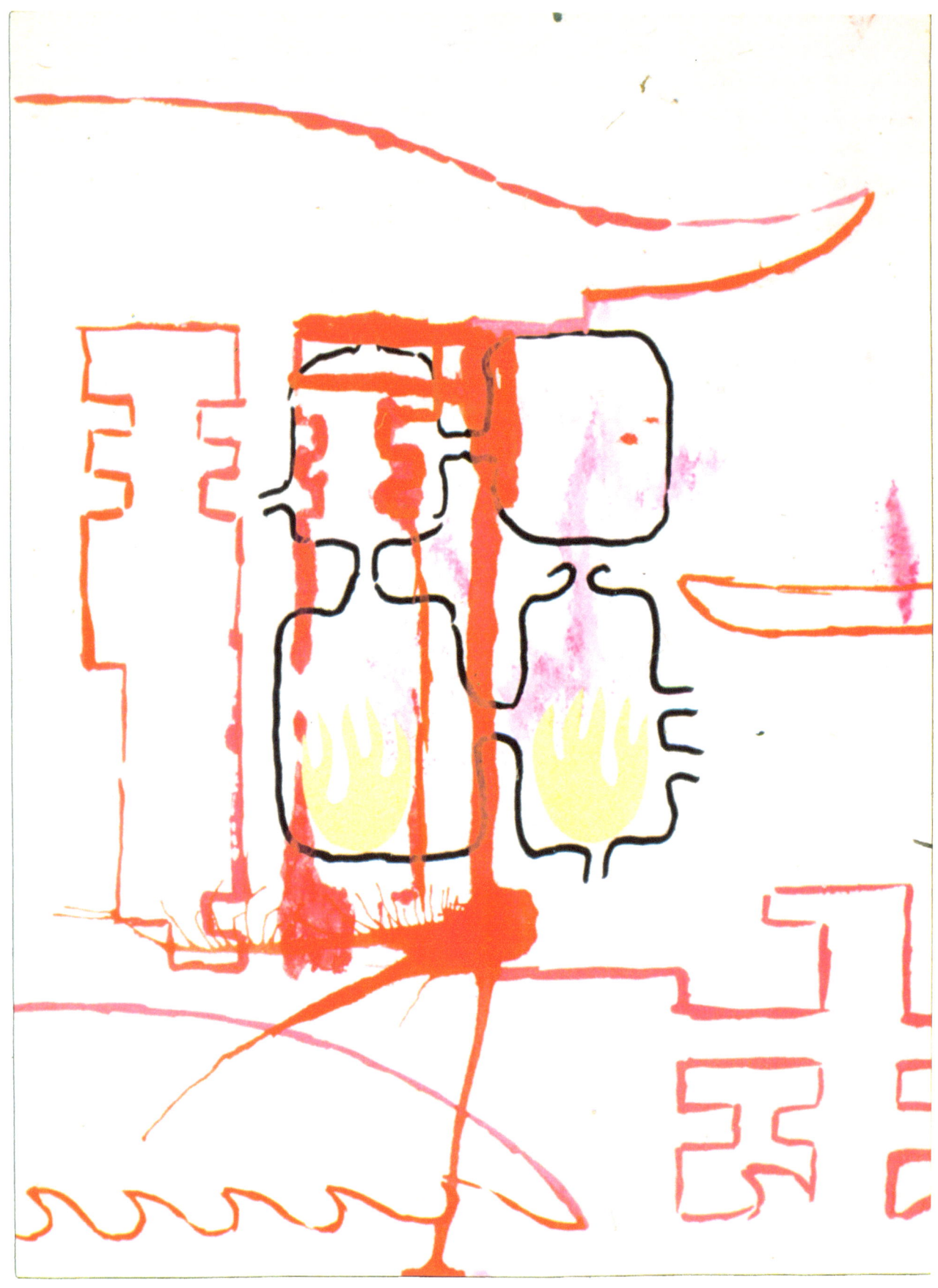

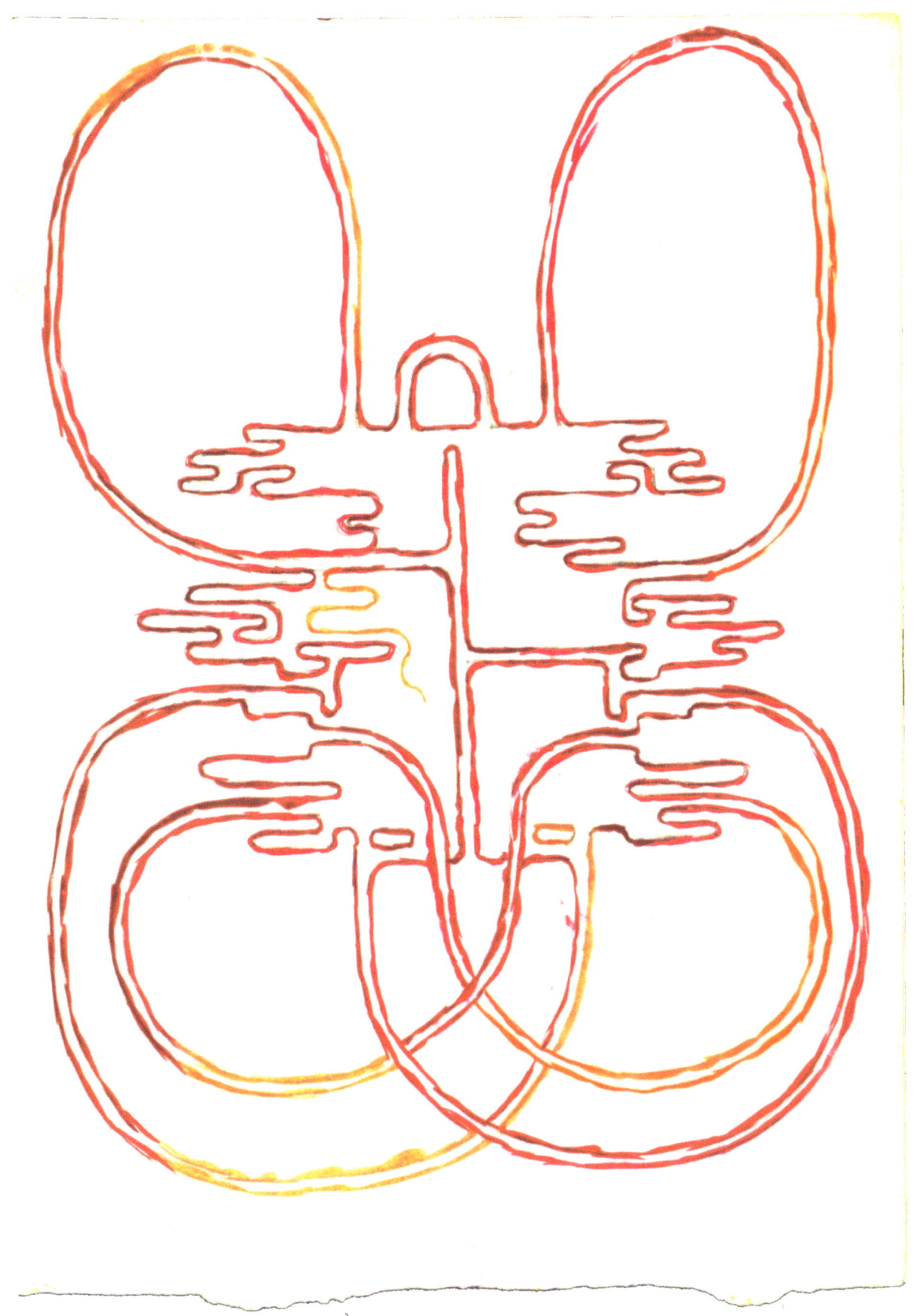

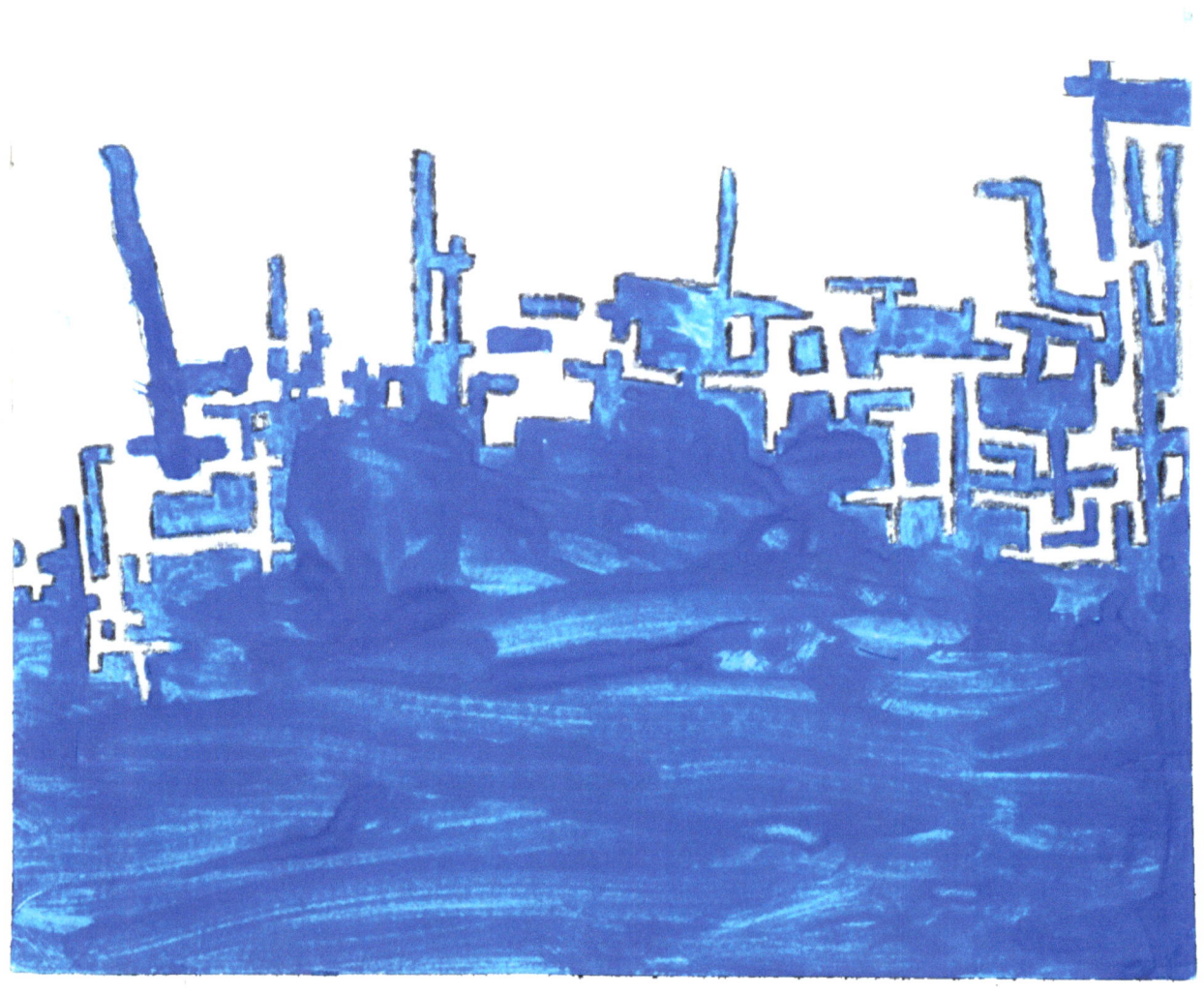

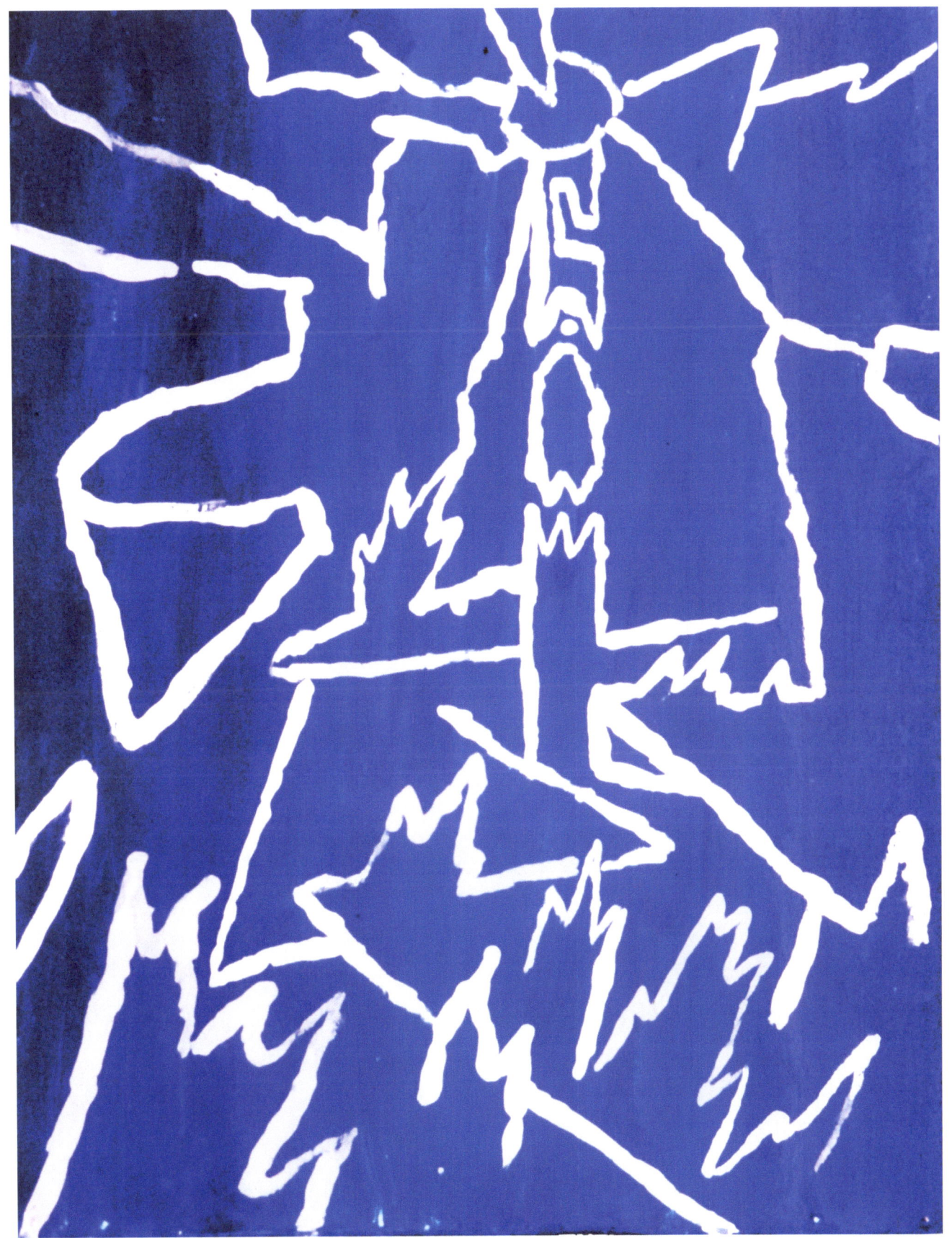

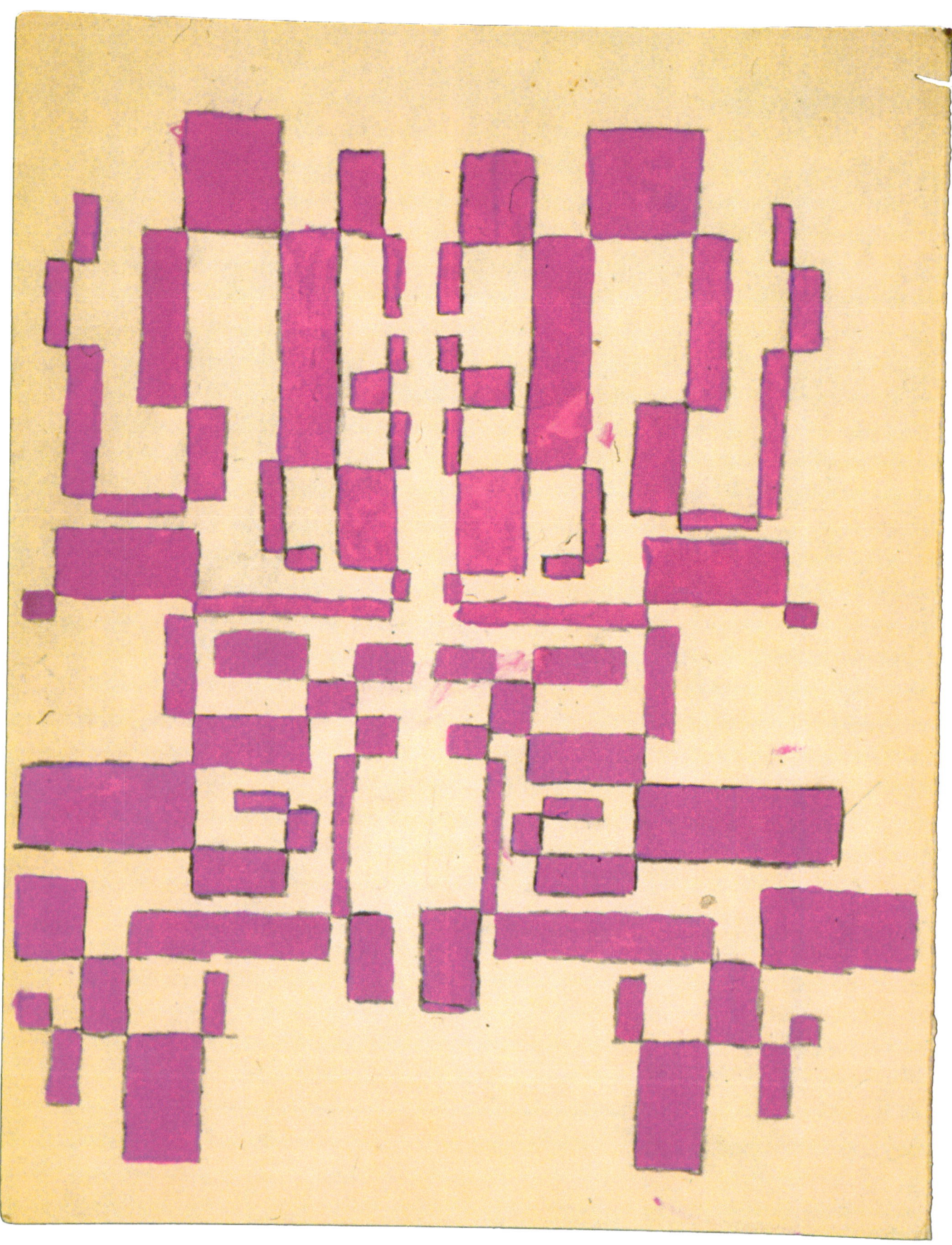

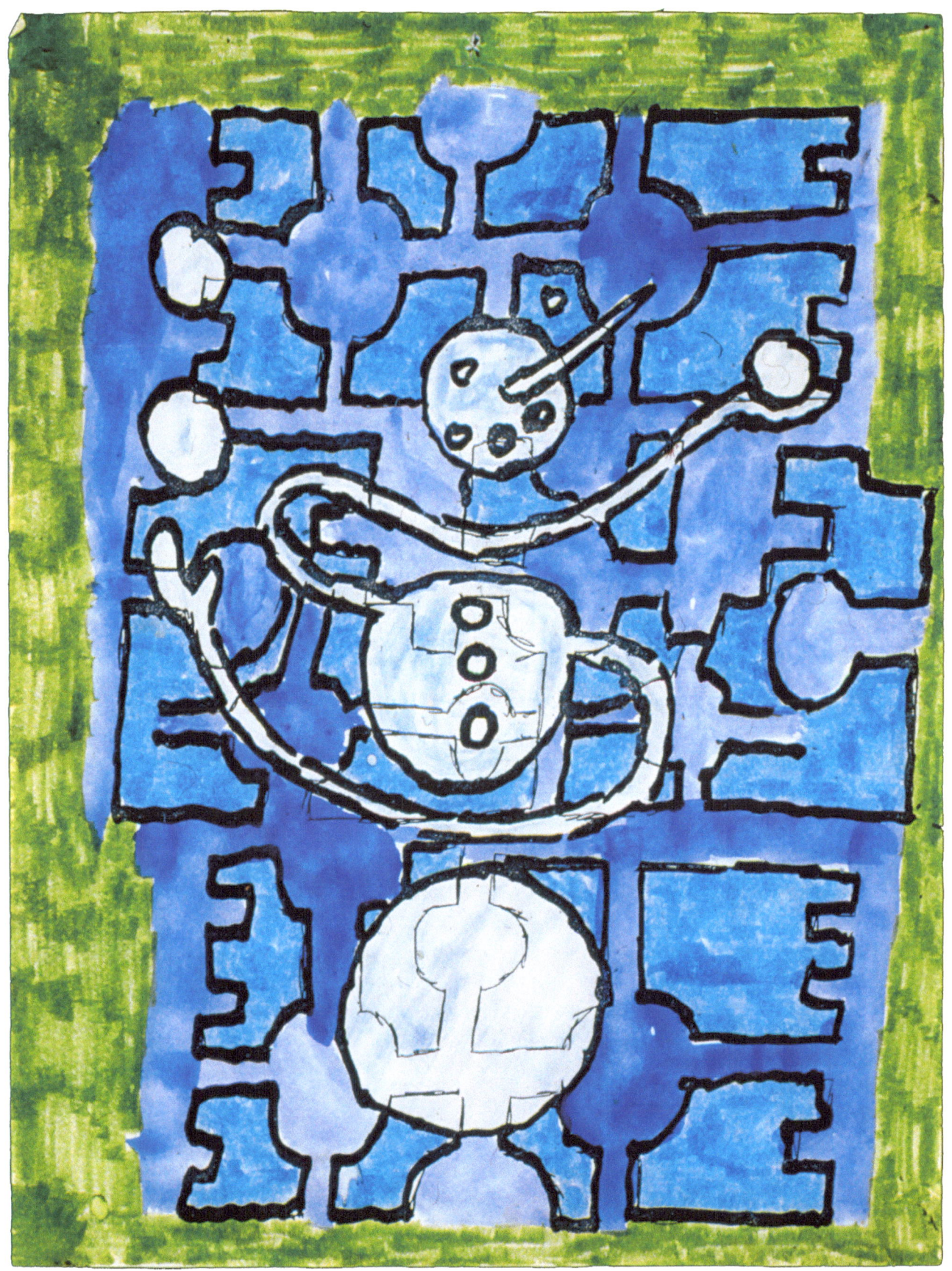

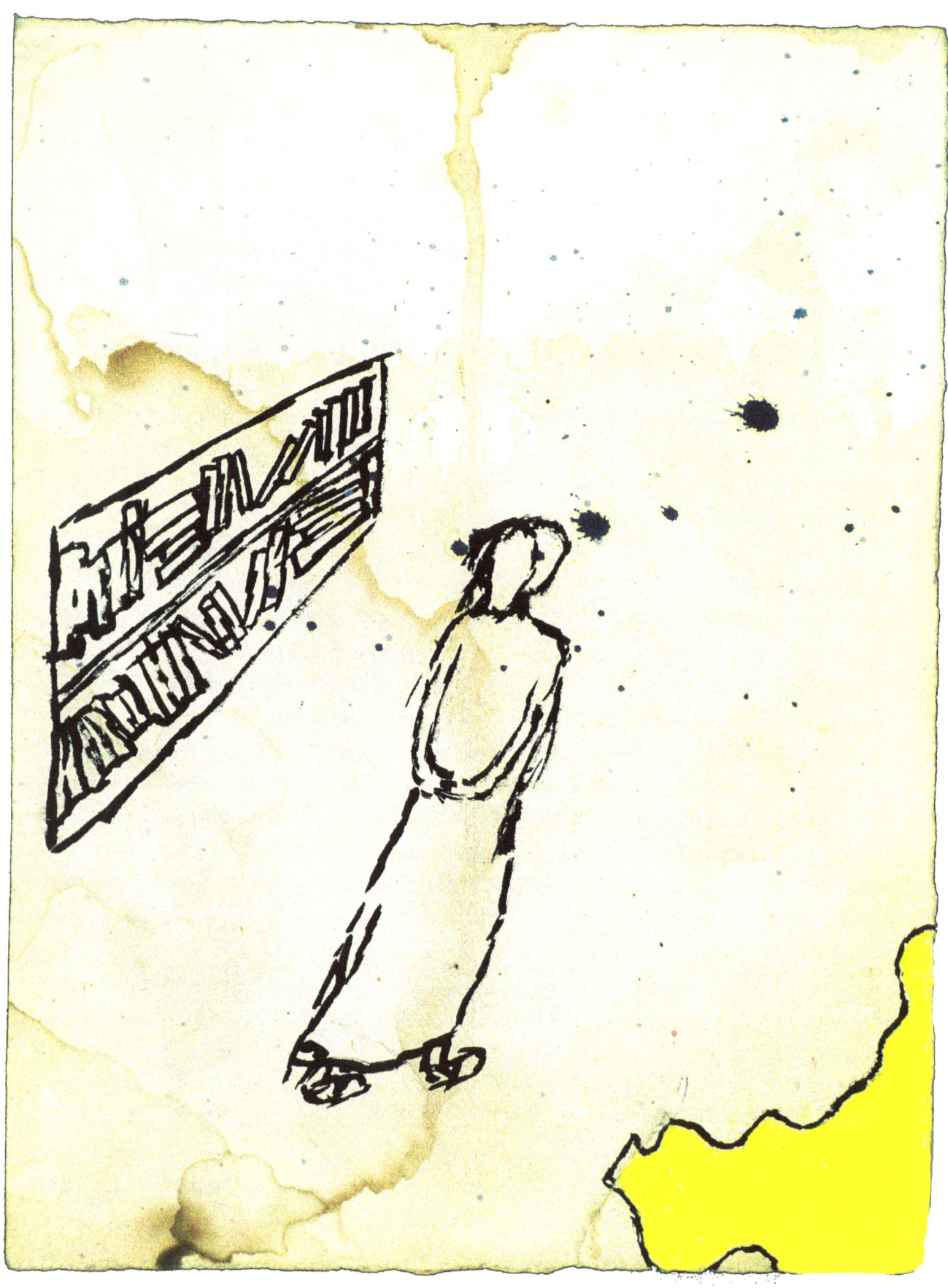

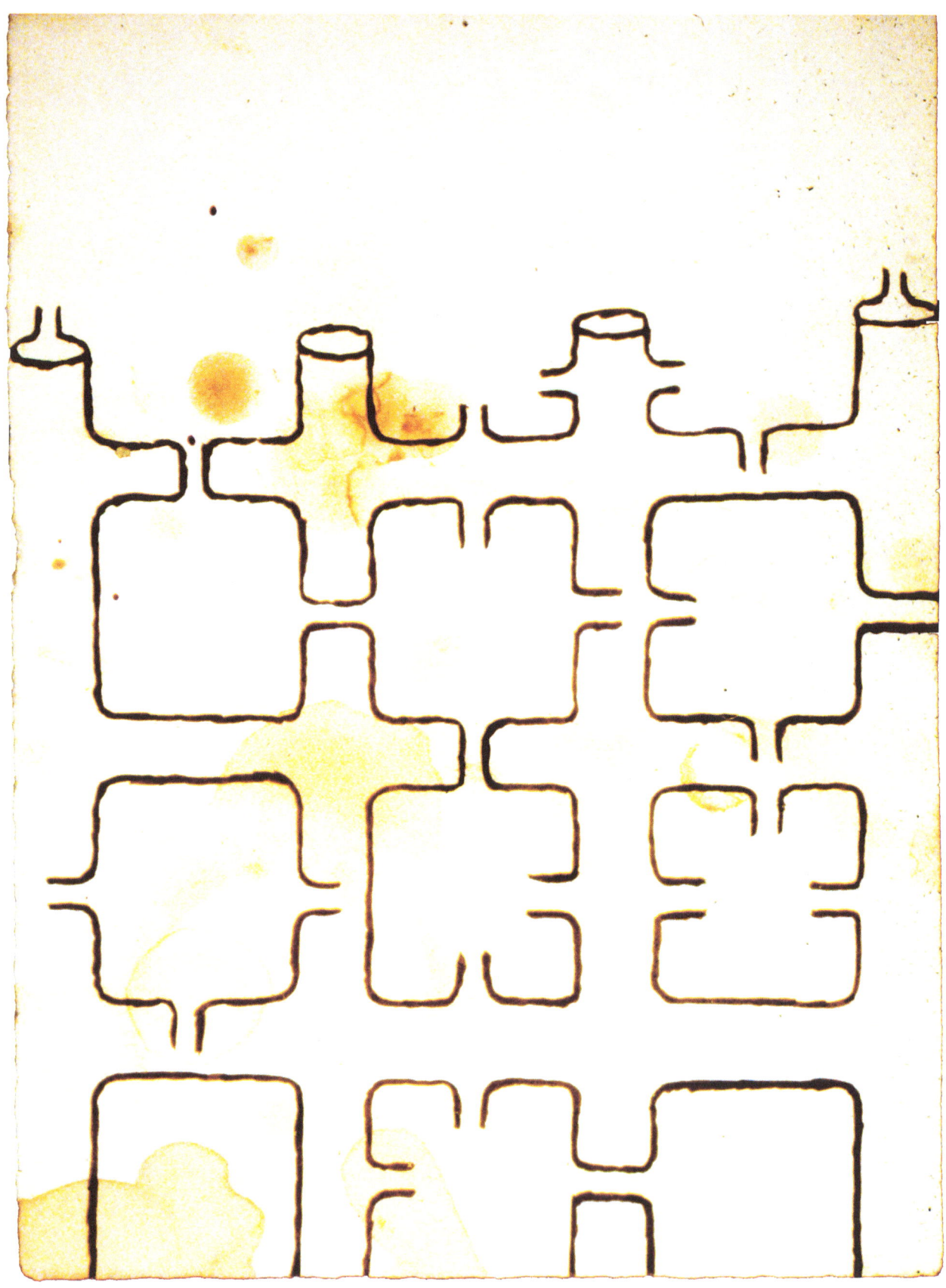

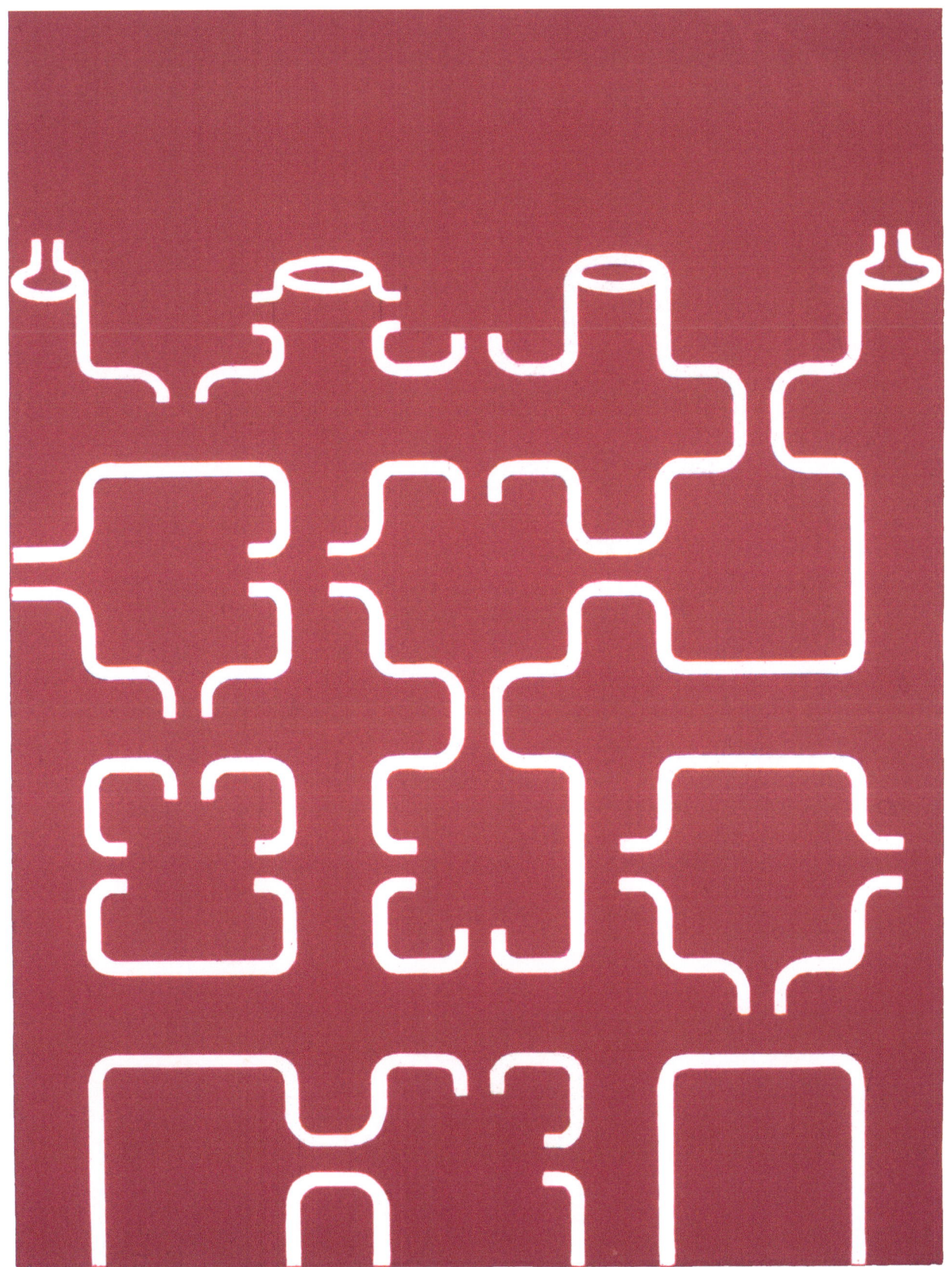

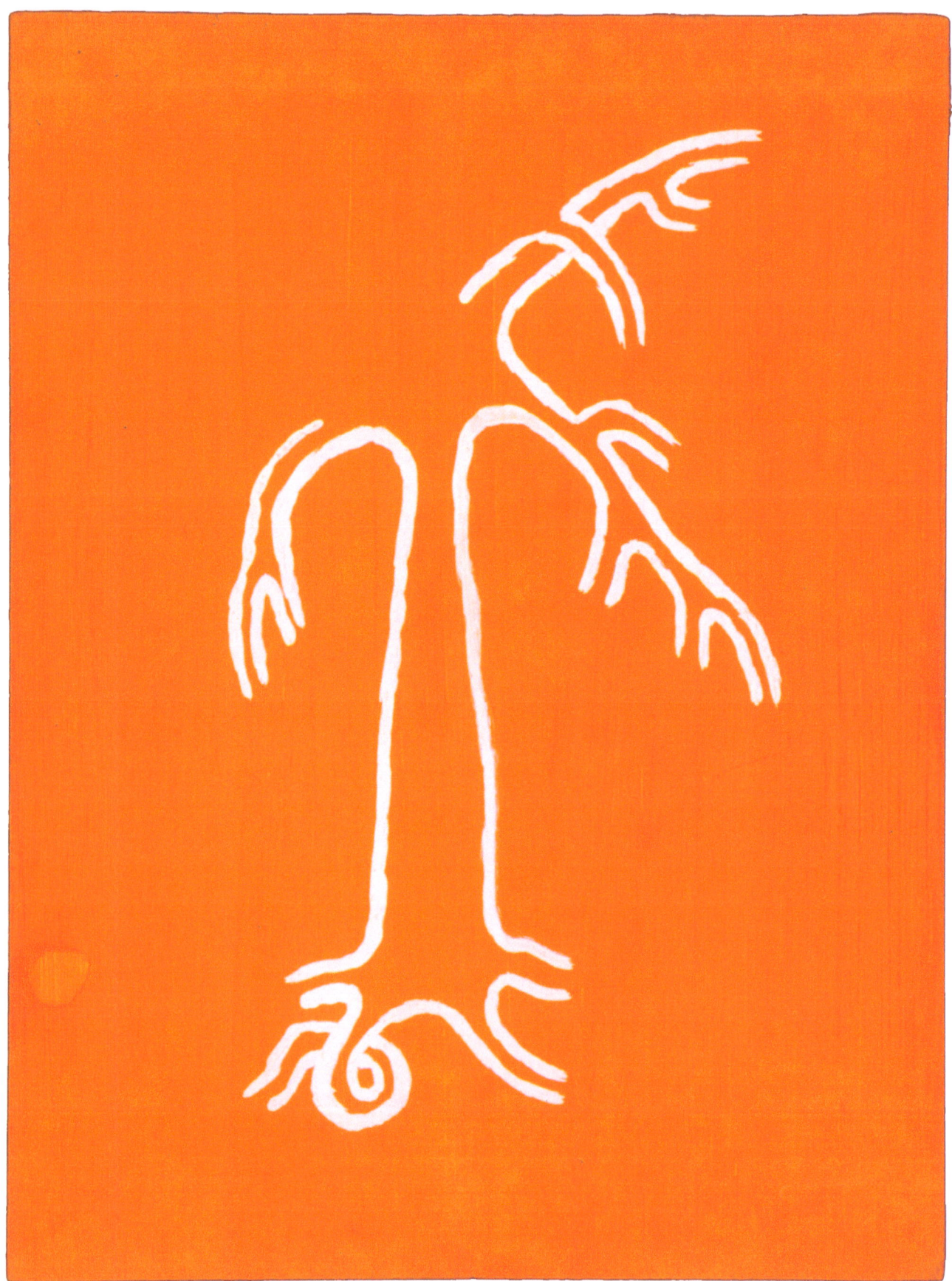

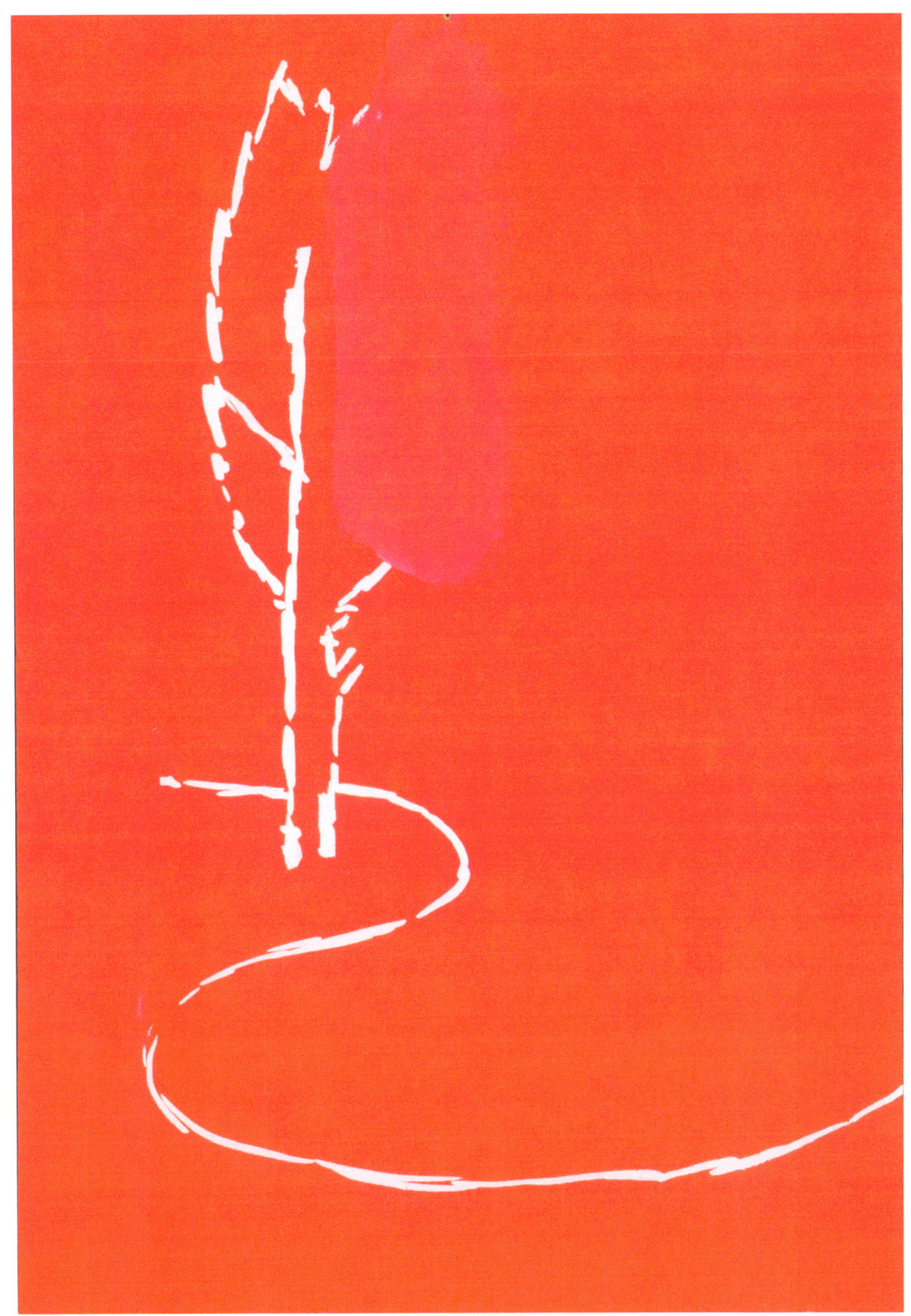

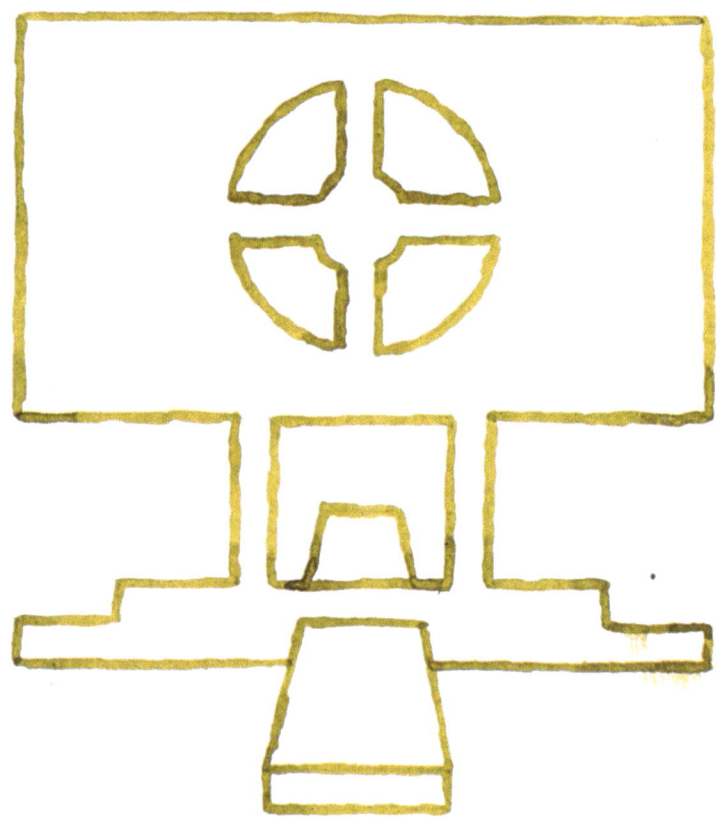

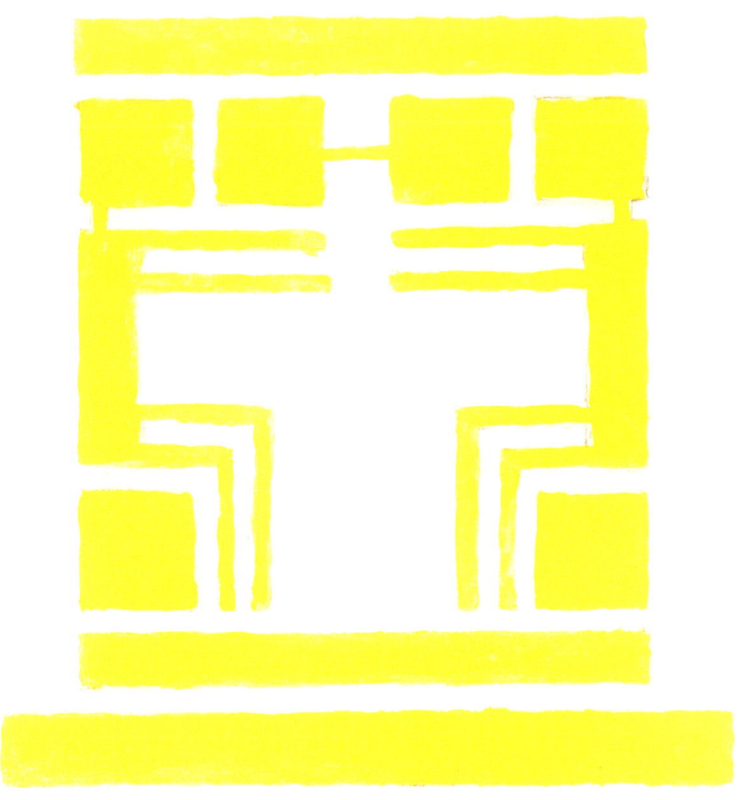

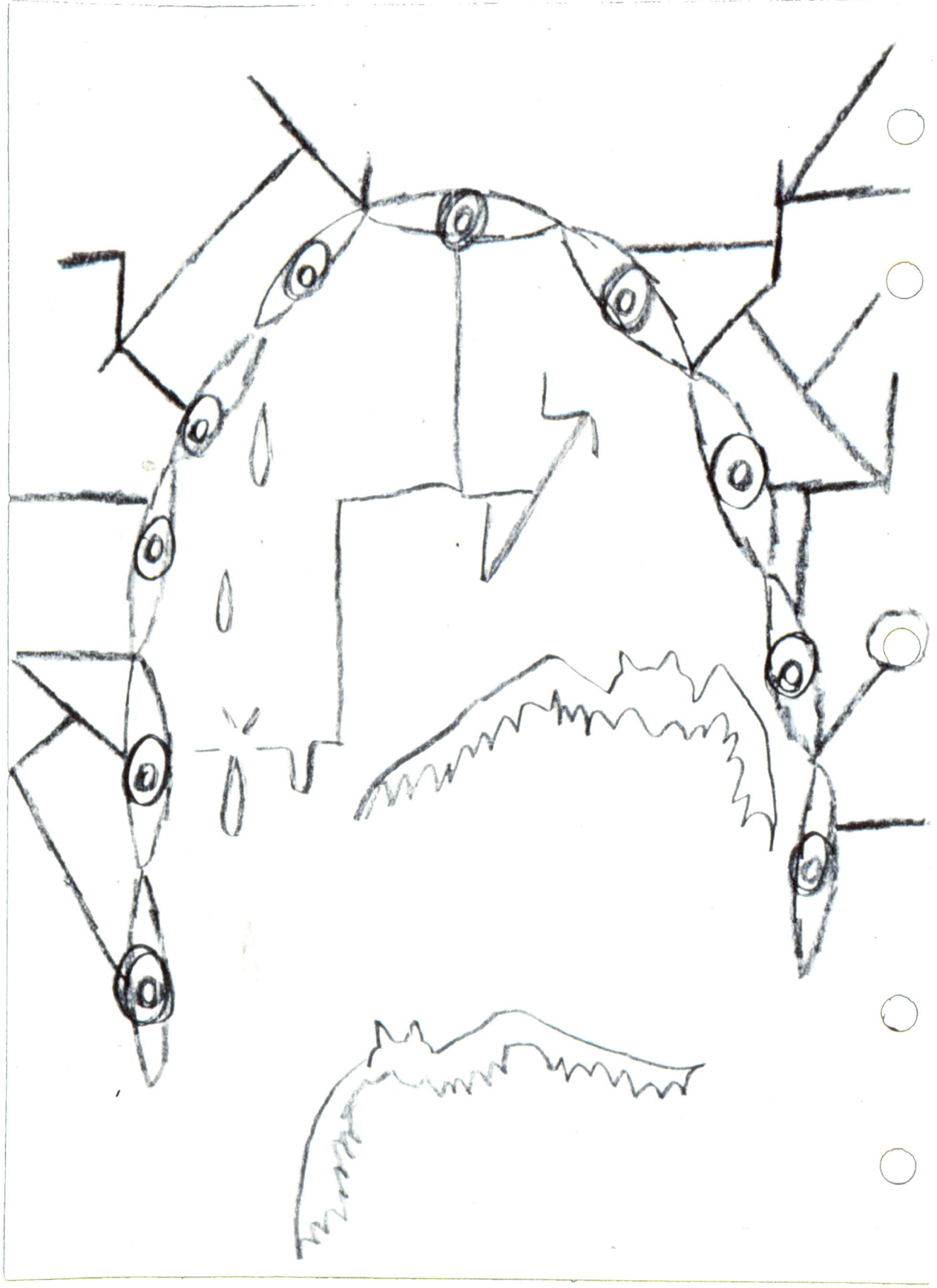

32

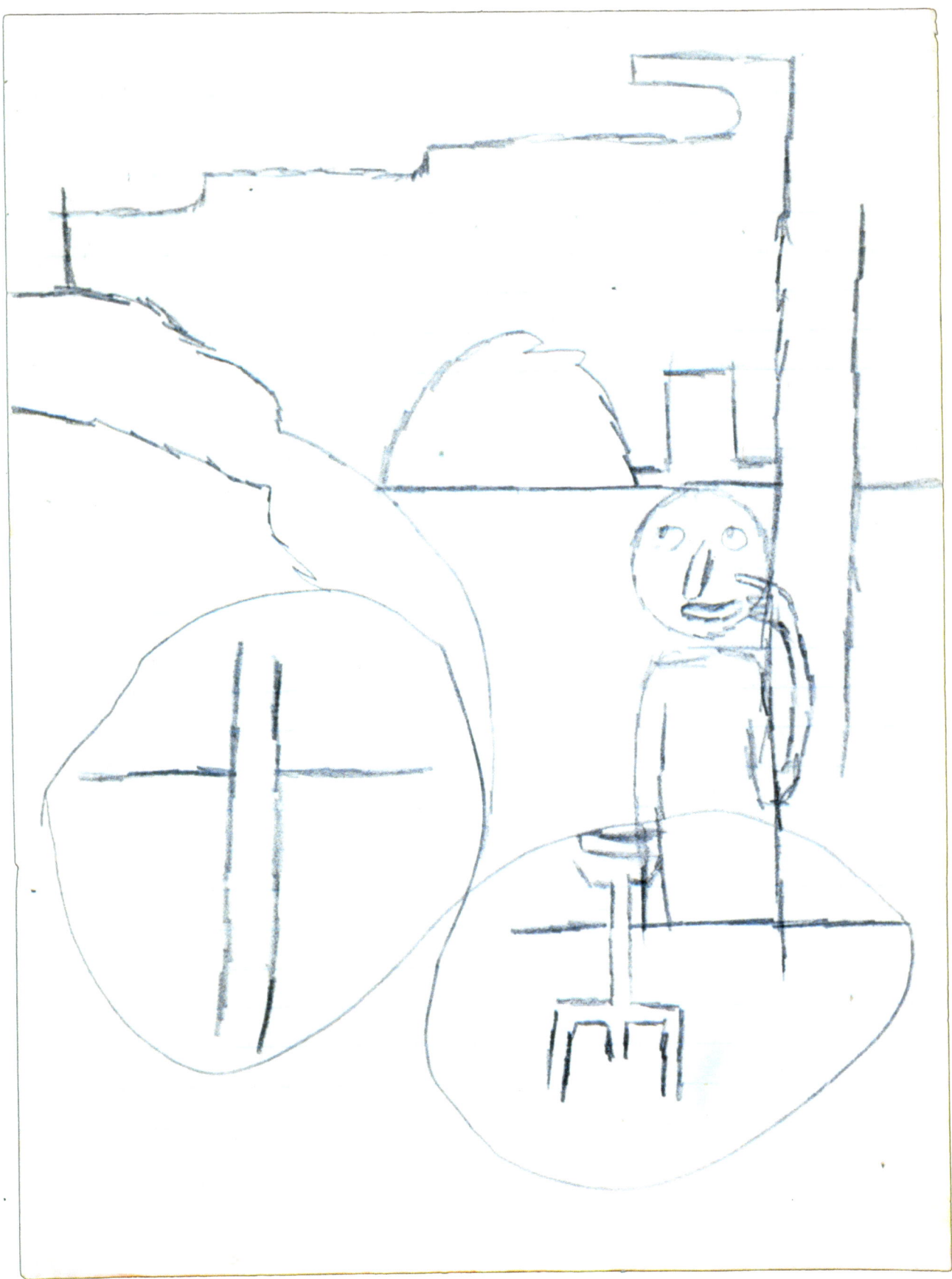

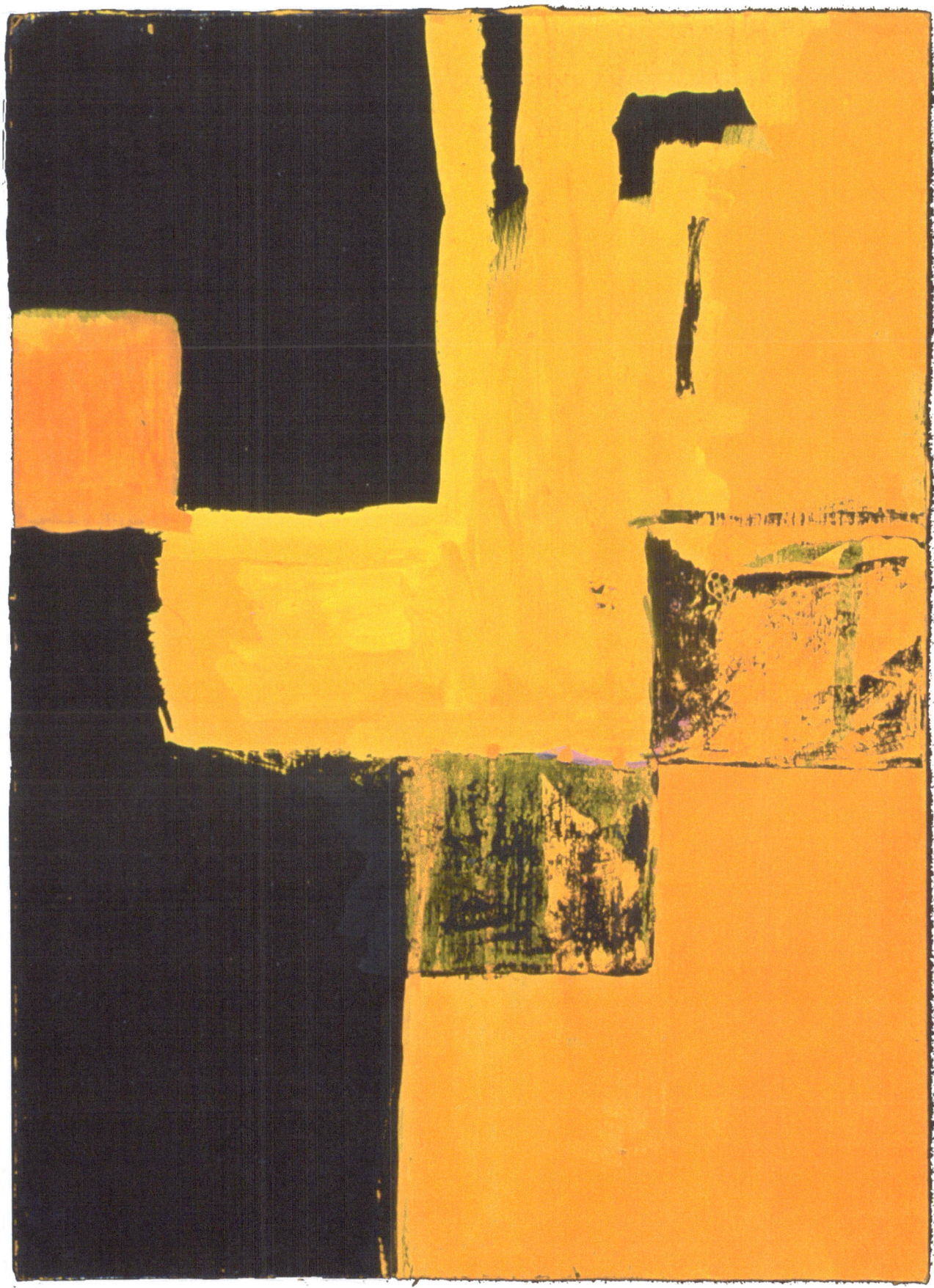

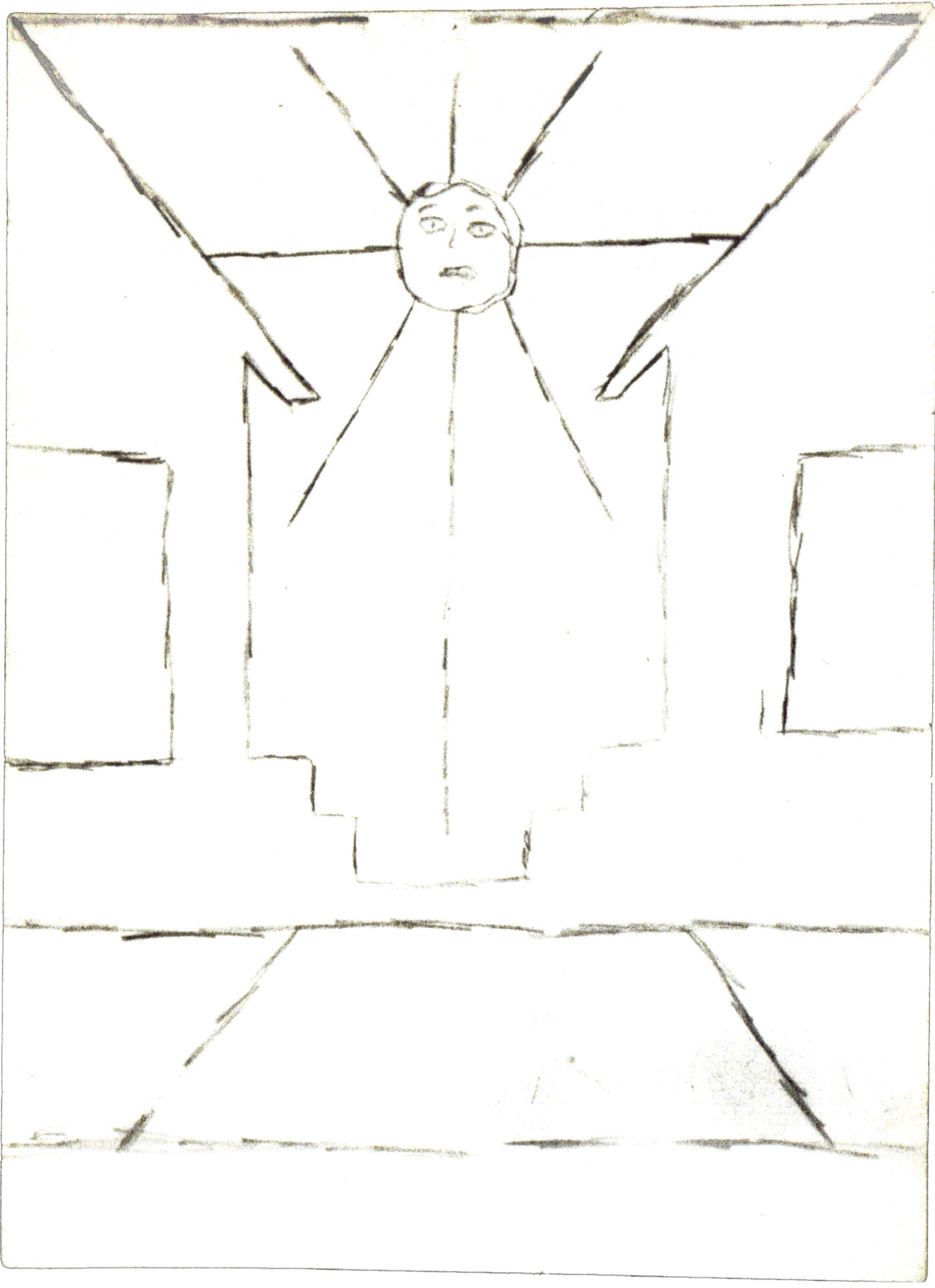

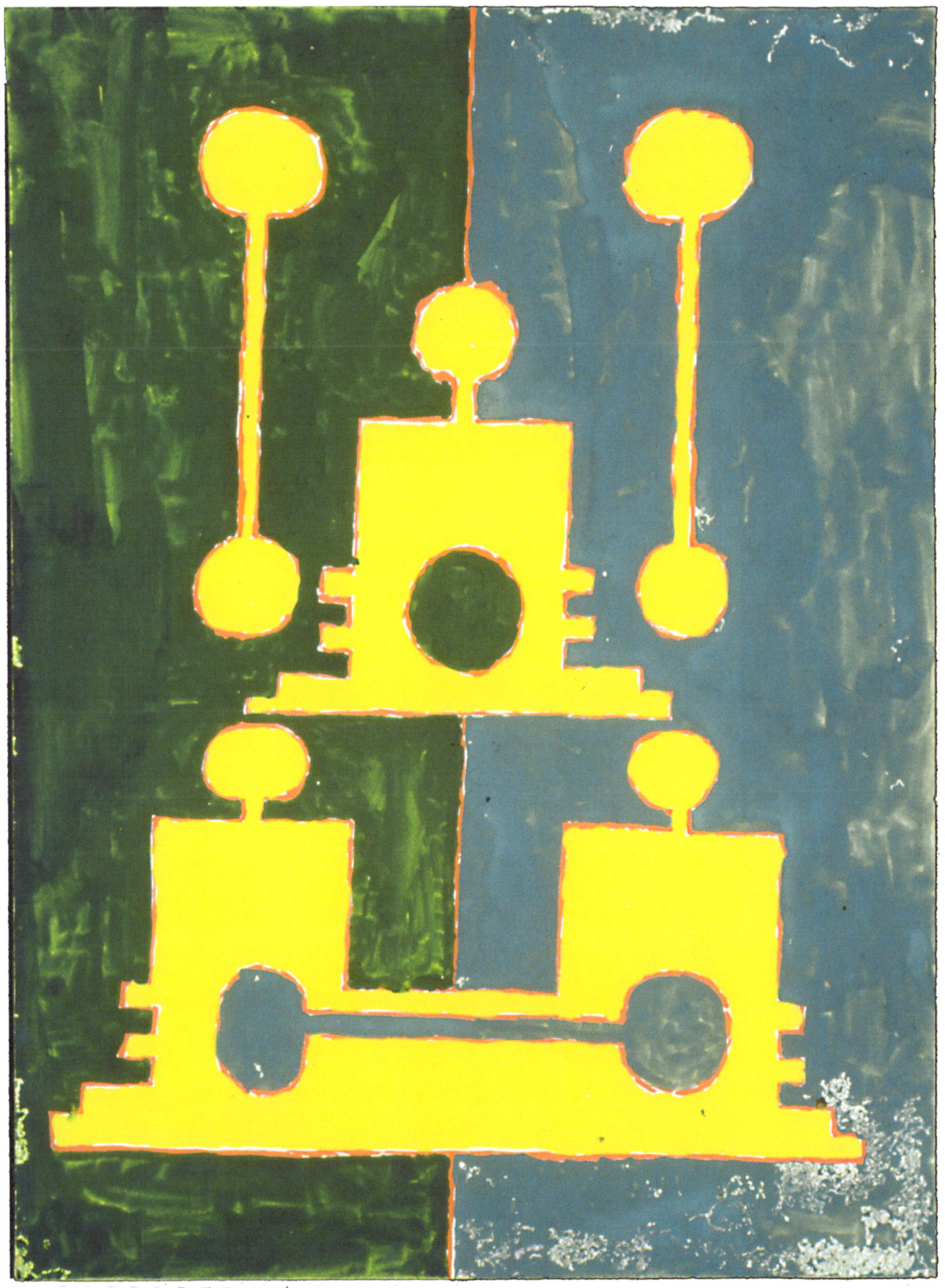

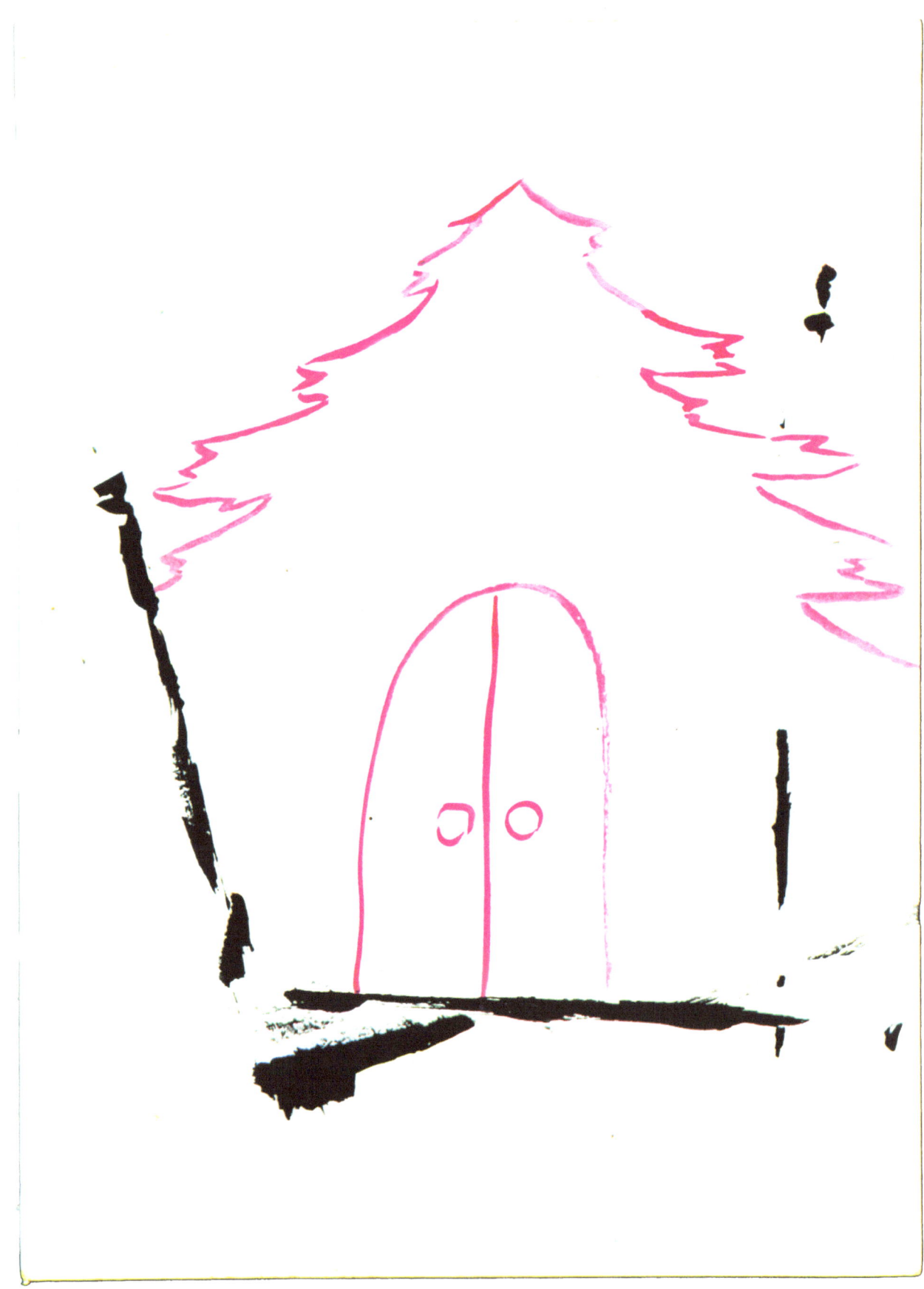

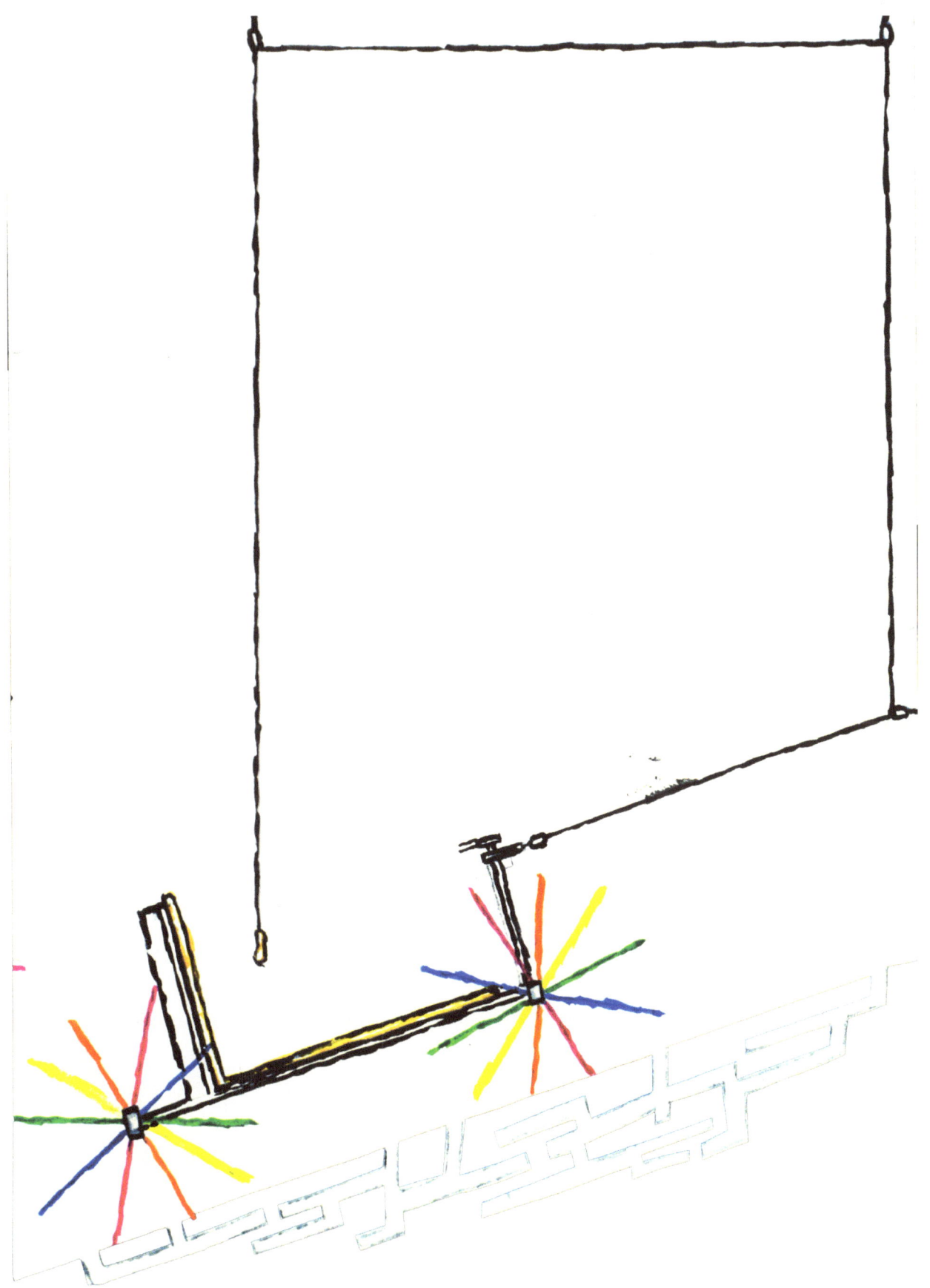

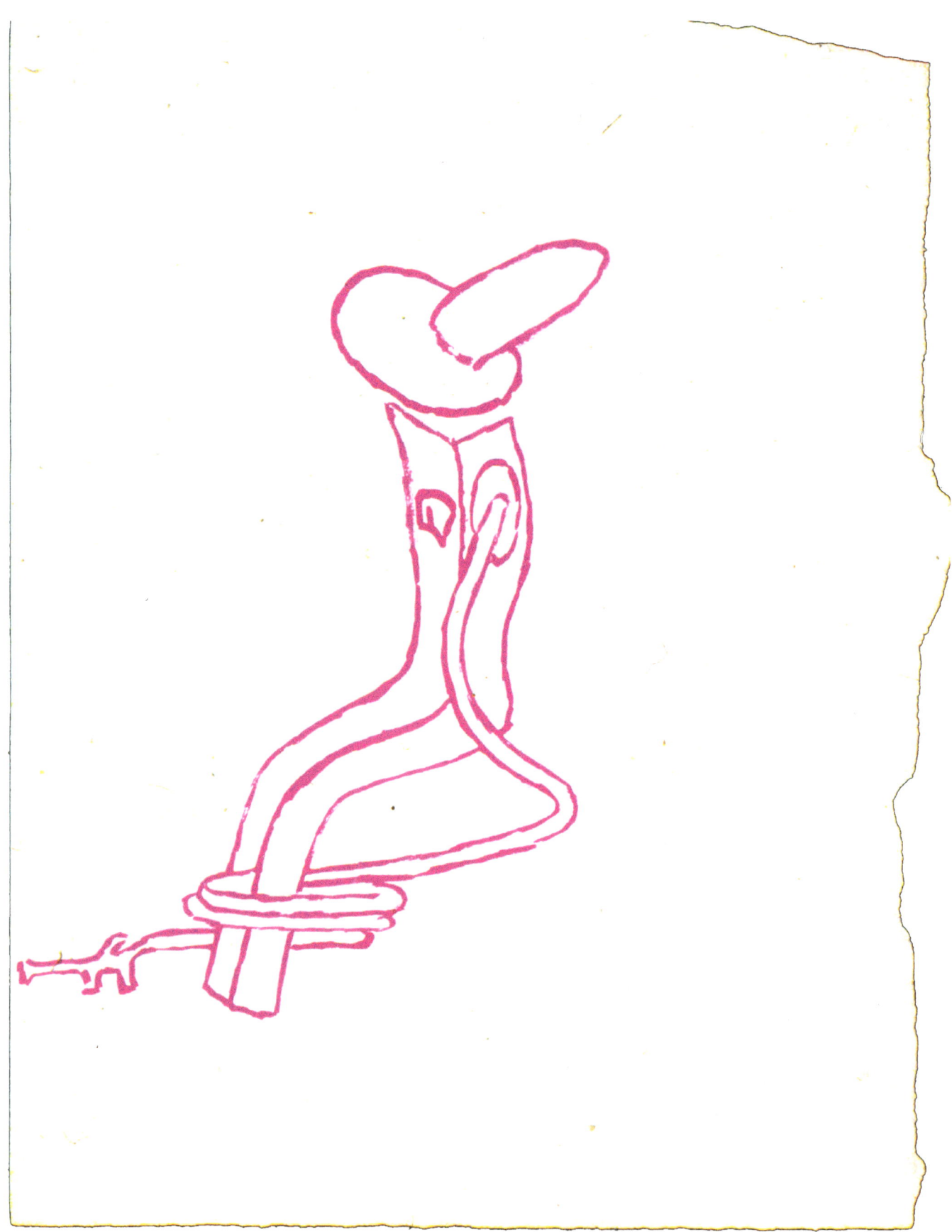

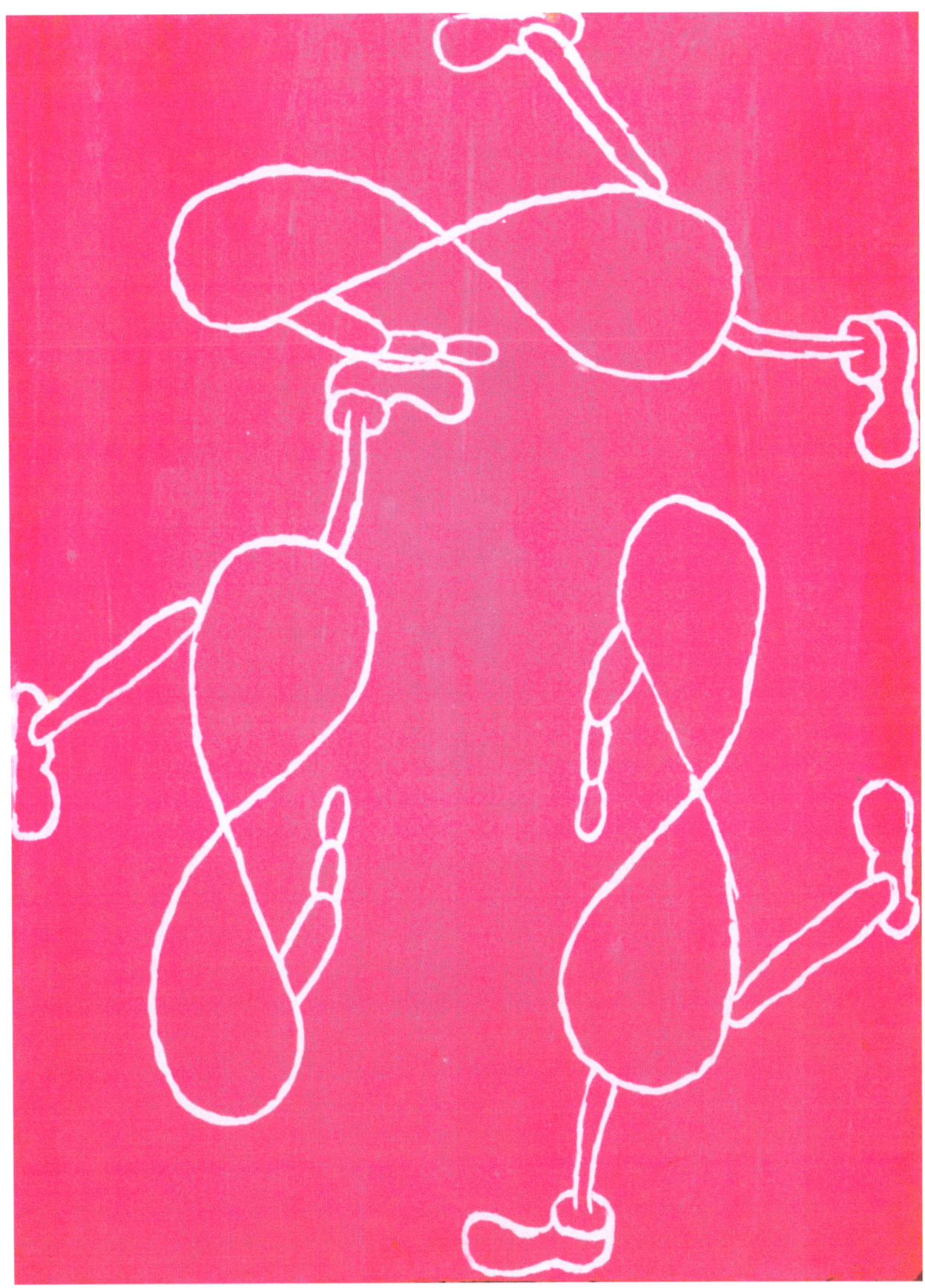

All drawings are approximately 9 x 12 inches.

1 *Miriam at Math*
pencil and gouache on paper, 1992

2 *Talking Pear*
(flopped) gouache on paper, 1987

3 *William the Pear*
gouache and ink on gessoed board, 1987

4 *Relationship Symbol Mirage*
watercolor and pencil on paper, 1988

5 *Study for a Lonely Gas Station*
pencil, ink, and gouache on paper, 1987

6 *Butterfly Boy with Ghosts*
pencil and gouache on paper, 1998

7 *Ghost with Whip*
China marker, ink, and gouache on paper
1989

8 *Fortress*
flasche and gouache on gessoed wood,
1989

9 *Dutch Door 2*
gouache on paper, 1989

10 *Fourteen Suns*
ink on paper, 1991

11 *Mischief Suns*
gouache on paper, 1994

12 *Bad Luck in Bahia*
pencil and gouache on paper, 1993

13 *Four, Five, Six*
pencil, pen, ink, and China marker on
paper, 1987

14 *Red Filter*
flasche and gouache on gessoed wood,
1989

15 *Castle Flood*
paper on paper, 1988

16 *Nazi Javelin Thrower Squinting in
the Sun*
gouache on paper, 1989

17 *Filter with Stone*
flasche and gouache on gessoed wood,
1989

18 *Detective at Red Castle Pier*
gouache, marker, construction paper on
paper, 1993

19 *Ghost Spade*
pencil and gouache on paper, 1992

20 *Cyan Sea*
pencil and gouache on paper, 1994

21 *Law*
flasche and gouache on board, 1986

22 *Magenta Two-for-One*
pencil and gouache on paper, 1992

23 *Bob the Snowman in Blue and Green Piece*
watercolor on pen and marker Xerox, 1986

24 *Jesus and Bookcase*
gouache and coffee on paper, 1992

25 *Three Burn*
pencil, marker, and burn on paper, 1993

26 *Fence/Filter with Coffee Stains*
gouache and coffee on paper, 1987

27 *Red Violet Fence/Filter*
flasche and gouache on gessoed wood, 1989

28 *Orange Tree*
flasche and gouache on gessoed board 1987

29 *Red Tree*
gouache on board, 1986

30 *Mind Symbol Billboard*
pencil and ink on paper, 1990

31 *Relationship Symbol with Two Seated Figures*
pencil and gouache on paper, 1985

32 *Threshold of Tears with Bats*
pencil on paper, 1987

33 *Man with Sun, Hat, and Cane*
pencil on paper, 1987

34 *Jupiter Makes Six*
pencil and gouache on paper, 1993

35 *Orange Clown Face*
ink and gouache on gessoed board, 1988

36 *The Mothers-in-Law*
pencil on paper, 1986

37 *One Soul and Relationship Pictograms in Green*
marker and gouache on paper, 1992

38 *Lochbaum*
gouache on paper, 1991

39 *Couch with Rainbow Wheels*
pencil and gouache on cut paper, 1993

40 *Gas Pump with Sombrero*
gouache on paper, 1987

41 *Crazy Eights*
flasche and gouache on board, 1988

Carl Vierow's drawings, like poetry, are worked
out thoughtfully and over time. Packed with back-
stories, personal symbols, schematics and maps to a
structure of his imagination, each is emphatically
meaningful to him. For us they are messages left
behind, like pictograms on a wall or a note for us to
decipher and ponder. Apparently simple, they reveal
themselves slowly, giving us clues to a perception
of a reality different from the one we know.

Carl Vierow lives in Bayonne, NJ.

Very great thanks to Matthew Droege for his kindness
and mastery fabricating some of these images. Very
great thanks to editor Jim Pustorino for the hours and
technology and encouragement needed to make this book.
Very great thanks to Jill Scipione for her help with
editing the images. Very great thanks to Nathalie and
Stephanie Velez for their kind help with technology.
Very great thanks to Jennie Russell for the photo. —CV

NEW DRAWING presents series of innovative, current
images from artists whose work explores the visual and
conceptual language of drawing.

VICTORY HALL PRESS is a division of Victory Hall Inc.,
a not-for-profit arts organization producing
exhibitions, events, education programs, public
projects and publications, based in the NJ/NY area.

Visit our website at www.victoryhallpress.org

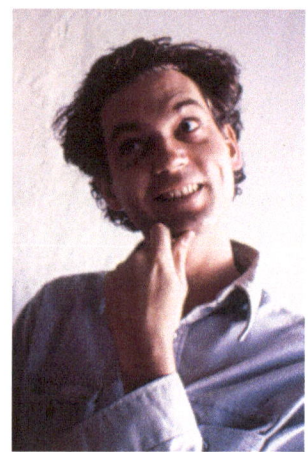